My
High Adventures
behind the
MOVIE SCENES

A Memoir of
RENE VELUZAT

PAGE PUBLISHING, INC.
Conneaut Lake, PA

First originally published by Page Publishing 2020

ISBN 978-1-6624-1861-7 (pbk)
ISBN 978-1-6624-1862-4 (digital)

Printed in the United States of America

To see more interviews and videos of Rene Veluzat and exciting videos of Blue Cloud Movie Ranch, go to Veluzat.com.

Links to YouTube videos and interviews:

The Controller—Behind the Scenes
"Rene Vehicles"
https://youtube.com /u ORPT6yMnAm

The Controller—Behind the Scenes
"Blue Cloud Movie Ranch"
https://youtube.com/tv 25bHyZg58

The Controller—Behind the Scenes
"The Cave"
https://youtube.com/npXFuVgzRDU

2011 Ken Scott—Blue Cloud
https://youtube.com/-1410JesxAw

Air Soft—John Lu
https://youtube.com/mm4R3CCzOHI

IMDB—Rene Veluzat

THIS BOOK IS dedicated to my wife, Patti Smith Veluzat, and my son, Marcel Rene Veluzat. Without their patience and help, this storybook would not have been possible to write. I love you both. Thank you.

Contents

A Special Thanks to My Wife, Patti Smith Veluzat

A VERY SPECIAL thanks to my wife, Patti Smith Veluzat. This is both a third marriage for each of us. After my other two very large weddings, which only lasted seven years each, we decided to get married in Las Vegas and had our few best friends attend the wedding in the Little Brown Church. Well, third time must be the charm as we are approaching forty years of marriage this year. We have one beautiful son, Marcel.

Patti was told she would not be able to have a baby. Well, miracles do happen. Marcel Rene Veluzat, our son, is now the ranch manager of my movie ranch Rene's 50's Town, a very successful small-time town set.

Patti owned her own business, Santa Clarita Valley Escrow. She had her business, and I had my movie business. She does not tell me how to run my movie business, and I do not tell her how to do an escrow. She has her own bank accounts and income, and I have mine, then we have our joint account.

She has her Mercedes, and I have my fleet of antique, exotic race cars, Hummers, and motorcycles. I think this makes a good marriage. Writing this book, *My High Adventures behind the Movie Scenes*, I could not have done this project without her help. So thank you, Patti. I love you.

Acknowledgments

To ALL OF you who supported my journey in the motion picture industry, thank you.

Special thanks to the following:

JAG TV series
> David James Elliott
> Catherine Bell

NCIS TV series
> Mark Harmon, star
> Mark Horowitz, executive producer
> Mark Shields, executive producer

Studio drivers, Local 399, my sisters and brothers and all crew people in the industry
Location managers
Fire safety advisers (FSA)
Tracy Danielson, for all your support through the years and your encouragement to write this book.
All pyro technicians, we had a "blast."

Blue Cloud Movie Ranch
> Dylan Lewis
> Frank Gardner, manager

Neal Hickerson, thanks for all your help and support.

Tony Meric, Tony Picture Car Rentals
David Wang, Army Trucks and Tanks
Ken Ziegler, Military Equipment Studio Rental
DEI
> Randy Dickinson
> Brad Dickinson

State Farm
    Tarrell Florent, CHFC agent
    Jeri Okamoto

Frank and Gayle Laza, Central Coast Electric Boats, Oxnard, California

My real estate team
    Tarlena Owens, CEO/CET, Federal Escrow Inc.
    Gail Kopp, Realty Executives
    Greg Maas, Realty Executives
Rebecca Locke, Coldwell Banker

Wells Fargo Bank
    Kammie J. Larsen, brokerage associate
    Wayne Simpson, financial adviser
    Michael John Turner, mortgage consultant
    And *all* the Wells Fargo Bank staff

Storm Larsen and Company

    Ragnar Storm-Larsen, master of business administration, thank you for all your help through the last forty-five years.

Law offices of Lynch and Lynch LLP

My doctor team
    Jacque Brooks, CFNP
    James Lee, MD, FACC, FSCAI
    Michael G. Quon, MD
    Nimit Sudan, MD
    And all the wonderful nurses and staff who work in these doctors' offices

Jason Crawford, marketing and economic development manager for the city of Santa Clarita, thank you for supporting me and my movie ranches through all the years. It has been a long road from then to now.

City of Santa Clarita Film Office and staff
    Jennifer Jzyk
    Matthew Curran

All the great members of the Pacific Corinthian Yacht Club and staff in Oxnard, California

Sally Culver Brownlow, for your encouragement to write this book.
Jim Bizzelle, thank you for your support.

Christina Veluzat, my wonderful daughter-in-law
Marcel Rene Veluzat, my wonderful son, I could not be without your help all the time.
And also my wonderful grandkids—Logan Kash Veluzat and Holland Victoria Veluzat

I love you all.

CHAPTER 1

Tom Cruise

Behind the Scenes

WHAT A STORY this is! I got a call from a Paramount location manager that they wanted to scout my movie ranch.

"Okay, this is good. What day and time do you want to come?"

We set a time for a week later. Who was coming? Tom Cruise was flying in a helicopter. OMG, a real megastar. Now I know the movie stars are just people like us, but he has made it and is megafamous. So I got megaexcited because he has had the talent to make it big-time. I give him all the credit in the world.

So for Tom Cruise, or any other star, I started to prepare for his arrival. I looked at my hands that were rough and thought, *How can I shake his hand with these?* So I started to work on my hands to try to get them clean and soft. Some stars would not shake hands, but I was hoping it would be different with Tom Cruise. So for the next week, I washed my hands a lot and put lotion on them to soften them up and then wore gloves.

Okay, the day had arrived for the scout and the helicopter to arrive. Prior to this, I had taken every precaution there was so there would be no trouble in landing and excessive dust. I took a water truck and wet down all the dirt around the landing zone that I designated as a landing spot for Tom. I planned on asking to take a picture with him when he landed. After all, I was the owner of the movie ranch. What could he say? No? Well, that would be okay too.

Then came the helicopter, and it made a perfect landing; no dust or rocks flew around the helicopter. Motor and blades shut down, and the door opened. Tom Cruise stepped out, stretched, and looked around. When he saw me, he asked if I was the owner. I said, "Hi, Tom. I am Rene Veluzat. Nice to meet you." Now the test began. I reached out to shake his hand, and he reached out and shook my hand. From that point on, I felt more confident. Tom said "Let's see the Mexican town" as we walked and talked with him and the other producers to the set.

Tom was directing this episode of the *Fallen Angels* for Paramount Pictures. Tom was impressed with the set. He asked me to walk alongside him so I could answer any questions he had. He had a lot of them, and I answered all of them, saying, "Yes, you can do that. Yes, you can paint, remove, destroy, blow up, whatever you need."

As the long scout was coming to an end, Tom said to me, "You certainly are a yes-man."

I said to Tom, "I am, and I am here for you to make your movie. As you know, it is called the Volkswagen effect. You can blow it up or destroy it as you will rebuild it ten times better than it was and make it look like a Rolls-Royce."

He looked at me, smiled, and said, "Thank you."

One of the producers said, "Okay, that is a wrap on the scouting, and we are out of here."

As we walked back to the helicopter, I was trying to figure out how to ask for that picture. As we got to the helicopter, I told myself, "It is now or never." After all, he talked to me all day and was very friendly and shook my hand. So I said, "Tom?" All the producers stopped to look at me. I knew they were thinking, *What the hell does he want?* I said, "Tom, do you think I could get a picture of you?"

The producers just laughed. Tom walked right up to my face about two inches away and said, "Rene, I don't think so." At that moment, I was devastated. I thought, *What the hell are you doing, Rene? He is a megastar, and he is not going to give you a picture.* Then he laughed and said, "Rene, not unless you are in it with me!" He asked one of the producers to take our picture. I was in shock; he was just teasing me.

I thanked him. They loaded up and took off as I was waving goodbye. I had that picture enlarged and had it hanging in my office along with many other pictures of stars.

Tom did come back to the ranch and filmed *Fallen Angels*. He said "Great shoot, no trouble" and thanked me again. What a guy!

I loved telling this story about Tom Cruise to my friends and at parties. My friends said, "You should write a book about your many stories. They are funny, and we like hearing how the stars really are."

It is still a thrill for me to meet the people who tenant the world of movies. I know the enormous pluck it takes to wedge oneself in among the legions of other hopefuls. I know that screen appeal is a rare and elusive trait. But the ability to occupy that narrow berth of working actors who consistently turn in exemplary performances is what really earns my respect.

In this business, I function as both a fan and a colleague. Working in entertainment is exercising the most extravagant level of make-believe. However, it is also a practice in the grim undertaking of making money. This industry, for all its reputation for frivolity, is built on discipline and proficiency. Only the sharpest survive. Therefore, as soon as I got the affirmative word, I launched into the preparation for Tom Cruise's arrival.

The first request they made of me was to arrange a landing site for his hired helicopter. I asked the name of the pilot because I needed to assess if the pilot recognized where our ranch coordinates were and if he knew where to land. I also did a check on his reputation. I did not want any old birdman bringing in seven location people onto my ranch without determining if he could be entrusted to do the assignment correctly and safely. Crashes and burns were on the far side of probability, but they were also a sober reality. I was also very sentient of legal suits. I tried very hard not to be sued.

Fortunately, the helicopter pilot was one I was familiar with. Mike Tambrou and I had flown together. He had also aviated in and out of my ranch a dozen times and was familiar with the lay of the land from routine. I made sure that he had the proper insurance policies and all the other protective niceties. We also established the frequency on which we were to communicate.

As I surveyed the landing pad, I rendered forth all my experiences to supersede any possible mischance. I knew that there were near misses in all kinds of places, even under the most flawless conditions. Dirt flying in the face of the navigator, a rock that was in the way, skids misaligned because of gopher holes—all could provide the catalyst for disaster. The platform I groomed was free of pocks, bumps, or defects, the groundwork befitting a movie star's entrance.

I inspected the Mexican town and reviewed the aspects they would be mostly interested in. I built the town myself, drew it from inspiration. I have a feeling for architecture and know how the camera's eye turns to certain aspects. My early training in life was simultaneously in film and in construction. In this town were elements of both history and reverie. There were doorways and windows that created intimate frames, long shots of facades that were stunning in approach. It looked like a village in fantasy, vaguely Mediterranean, somewhere in time, a sun struck hamlet of mysterious quarters.

I checked to make certain that the moving parts moved and the solid parts remained stable. I designed the interiors to accommodate the gear and transient structures of moviemaking. Walls could be added, lights strung, dollies scurried, whole sections brought down by violent means, if that was what the shot called for. I allowed for paint, plaster, nails, and glue. It was merely a set, and any superficial activity to simulate a sense of period or place was permitted.

The Mexican town exteriors were also receptive to the old and new language of decoration. They had been enriched by details, texture, pattern, and paint finishes, cheating the eye with imitation and derivation in accordance with the art director's fancy and budget. I was not wedded to a determined look. The facades had been transmuted into barely recognizable forms in car commercials, sexy calendars, and the odd music video with their penchant for distressed veneers.

As the work proceeded, I liked to be on the set to make sure the company got everything they came to do. I liked the factors that I could govern to go well. I was the visionary, handyman, park ranger, technical consultant, and demigod rolled into one. I could control the town. At the end of the day, I wanted my provisions to be well received. If the ranch were not to perform well, then I would take it as a personal deficiency. But as long as I ran the town, it was, as the crude expression goes, "all tits."

When an inquiry was made of me, my favorite response was *yes*. My agenda was to facilitate any way I could. From all my years interwoven in this industry, I could make a judgment if a shot was plausible. It had to be safe first and foremost. If it caused permanent mine, I wanted to be compensated accordingly or the materials renovated back to prior condition. I knew the temperament of the land and all the edifices upon it. The town had been serrated brutally, filed upon, heavily doused with pitch and ash, through all variants of pandemonium, and yet it persisted to discharge its duties another day, because I knew the limits of its durability. My investment and livelihood depended on supplying a malleable substance.

I was briefed that Tom Cruise came to look at the big Mexican hotel on the hill. I tidied it by taking out every wee bit of trash, collected all the nails and screws that had been left behind, and swept it clean. To keep the dust down for the official review, I wet down the surrounding grounds moments before their arrival. Dust is part of the character of the sets, and many, like the Japanese, find it wondrous stuff. But for the members of Tom Cruise's scouting mission, I was determined to keep the flying debris out of their eyes and mouths.

This was not going to be the first impression. The procedure started with a group of location people taking pictures. They labeled their shots and took notes, which they presented to the producer, the director, the writer, and the production art designer with the rest of their findings. I had no idea Tom Cruise was part of the package.

One of the more important determinants during a text scout was backlight. Since the camera could not be shot into the sun, the director would position the sun behind the scene to light up the set. It would save hundreds of thousands of dollars in electrical lighting. When I built the town, I positioned the buildings according to the sun's path. Part of the town would get sun in the morning and the other in the afternoon. So the crew shot one portion at a time. Tire camera worked all day, following the light, using the energy of the Southern California sun. In the case of the hotel, it had the sun in constant company.

The hotel was a two-story affair with a dramatic staircase, balconies, deep ledges, archways, and grand moldings, with commodious interiors, and all built to code. Ordinarily, movies would build their own sets, but they would use marginal materials because it was cheaper and it would be easier to collapse and cart away. I constructed my sets using heavy, bulky materials, just as beefy as the substances of the housing trade. My buildings were assembled to be durable, with plaster, concrete, two-by-fours, beams, studs, everything, in order to withstand the assault of cosmetic changes.

The film companies would change the surface details during the prep days. They would set up contrivances that make it look unique. And then on their wrap days, they would alter what they have filmed their picture on the ranch. They would move out their trailers, their generators, their electrical lights, their cords, and their props, which was set decorating, camera cars, transportation cars. They would also refurbish the sets back to the original condition if I did not like the way they refitted them.

For the show that Tom Cruise eventually directed, there was nothing done to modify the surface details. The Mexican hotel especially pleased his exacting standards. They kept the Mexican tones of yellows, browns, and tans. They also chose to use the cantina at the bottom of the hill. In it they built ten different sets, bringing in their wild walls, which were temporary walls that stood up with back braces and were nailed into the floor so they held up. These wild walls were only eight feet tall so that the electricians could have the other four to ten feet with lights looking over the top to light the set. Or these wild walls could have two sides with a back wall and the crew looking into the front.

After I had received the contract, I was on set every moment Tom Cruise filmed his television episode of the *Fallen Angels*. I told him to find me if he needed anything. I would be radio distance away. At the end of the day, he thanked me, saying he had a great day. It was a great shoot because they never did have to find me again.

All day I had kept myself busy providing protection and surveillance. The producers had asked me to ensure that kids would not sneak onto the property and disrupt Tom Cruise's operation. This was understandable not only because he was a charismatic star who was frequently subjected to intense adulation but as this was his initial foray into directing. He did not want onlookers fracturing his concentration while he served his new discipline.

The show had their own security force, which I oversaw to make sure they were properly licensed. I also watched to see that they were not harboring some phony guy with a smuggled camera. I had my own patrol company, Titanium Protection, named after the strongest metal in the world because my aim was to provide the strongest protection to the stars, the crew, and their equipment. I set one of my guards at the gate and two guards walking and looking on the set to make certain no one was on a mountaintop with a big telephoto lens trying to take an unqualified shot of my special guest.

As ranch manager, I had been offered great sums of money from the tabloids to give illicit stories about stars taping here. It has never enticed me in the slightest. I wanted actors to feel free to range all over this beautiful place and enjoy the fresh air and the glorious chaparral and not have to hide in their trailers for fear they might get picked off by covert paparazzi.

The day Tom Cruise first came to the ranch, I designated a one-hundred-by-one-hundred-foot round landing area, which I delineated in a circle with red cones. With my four-thousand-gallon water truck, I wet down all the dust. Excess dust could be taken through the intake and cause the helicopter to choke out, possibly not have full landing power, and crash. I reconnoitered the area once again for bottle caps, tin can lids, or pieces of board. The smallest particle of trash could be sucked back into the rotor blades, causing them to go out of balance and turning the whole helicopter upside down in a dynamic rollover. So far, there had never been any fatalities on the ranch.

The coordinates were north of the San Fernando Valley, and finding the ranch was mostly visual. The pilot had to be at a four-thousand-foot elevation to skirt the electrical towers and the power lines. There were a thousand feet of line between the towers, and they were not very visible. The most likely worst-case scenario would be pilot error in not seeing the power lines and getting helplessly hung up in them.

Besides grooming the landing pad and the ranch facilities, I turned to my own personal preparation. When I was younger, I did hand inserts. These were close-up scenes of my hands doubling for the star's. For those shots, I wore the identical clothes and jewelry as the actor's while he was off preparing for the next scene. Before and between takes, I was instructed by the makeup people to coddle my hands with lotion and protective gloves. I wore the thin white cotton gloves used by the negative cutters.

These days my hands were not as pretty as they once were. And the day I got the call, I was engaged in the rough work of building something on the ranch. I looked at my hands, and they were a discouraging sight—bleeding, chapped, and coarse. My blessed mother had taught me that you only get one chance to make a good first impression, and I was my mother's son. I could not shake Tom Cruise's hand with the business end of a cactus paddle. So I embarked on an intensive hand rejuvenation program.

I scrubbed them until the pigment almost came off. I applied lotion as much as ten times a day. And I wore brown cotton gloves. This regime was not as simple as it sounds. My lotion was kept in the cab of my truck, and frequently, I was spotted by teamsters on the set pumping the bottle. In their macho way, they assumed I was washing my hands with gasoline. I let them think what they liked. The firemen, on the other hand, wanted to get into my truck and chop my leg off. People have always had a special fondness for me and like to trade tales. For the firemen, I gave an abbreviated version of my new preening habit and made self-deprecating jokes about it, not mentioning who the recipient of all this primping was for.

It was about ten in the morning when Tom Cruise alighted from his transport on a warm Indian summer day. Previous to the rendezvous, I had wet down the pad so it was neither dry and dusty or wet and muddy but desirably solid and firm. The blades were slowing down, and I saw him unlatch his seat belt. He strode confidently away from the spin of the cooling blades into the prepared area. I took a deep breath, wiped my hands of nervous sweat, walked over to him, and extended my greeting. He took my hand and shook it, then he smiled. Mission accomplished; normal handshake, with neither participants offering wet nor rough holds and done on steadfast ground.

I addressed him as due his station as Mr. Cruise. He then rectified me and asked to be called Tom instead. I happily complied.

I have been through the drill innumerable times before with other prospective clients. I would show the ranch, see what they wanted, show what they could do and what they could not do, see what they wanted to do or what they wanted to use or how long they would be there, and just help get the show organized for them. And then I would negotiate the contract with the location manager, and the clients were happy.

In this case, I knew that I would be doing the show. I just knew it. Tom really liked the Mexican town, and I really wanted his business. As was the case with all previous propositions, I would work with the producers, directors, and writers and give them anything they needed, anything they asked, within the realm of reason. When it came to the price, we would negotiate it out and split the difference. But I have never had a show come to me that I could not work out. Not one show. If they had five dollars or they had five million dollars, we would always hit on a happy medium. I have worked it out even with the student films. I have managed to work out within their perimeters and get them in and them out, and they were happy.

I had been managing the ranch for twenty-five years. I expected a barrage of questions, and they were always similar in scope. They deal with the technical aspects of filmmaking. But there were still the questions a tourist would make on an excursion trip. The town was so appealing with its graceful forms and organic vibrancy that it seemed impossible that it was not inhabited by people. I could see it in the filmmakers' eyes, the possibilities of setting up camp, discovering this place of mystery, living and working amid all this silence and beauty.

The primary question seemed to be how often the ranch worked. It was a game, a deft disclosure on my part. They were trying to find out how much exposure the ranch has had. If I said something vainglorious, like it was booked every day, then their enthusiasm would withdraw. Picture people do not want buildings that have been used repeatedly. They cannot abide their novel and creative operation be set before a long-worn, retread backdrop. And yet I must give the impression of value and considered capability. So I would say that though my family had owned it since 1940, it had not been a working motion picture ranch since the early seventies. The ranch worked all the time; however, it only worked in pieces all the time.

Which was the truth. When *Harper's Bazaar* magazine came to shoot a fashion spread in the late eighties, they captured the model close to the architectural elements, with lines of laundry and bunches of flowers and fruits to dress the sets. When a Japanese outfit came to pose a naked, lovely lassie, they set her on the lonely roads, passing through an unexpected shower of snow. The ranch was chameleon yet distinctly indelible. It would suit the visionary's quest.

The entire town had been shown on the movie *Extreme Prejudice*. They shot 180, which was everywhere, but when they edited the film and put it all together, they had lots of close-ups, but not an establishing panoramic shot that would identify it definitively.

It was not like nearby Vasquez Rocks, which had been filmed so habitually; it was the most common sight in television and movies. Vasquez Rocks, that slanted, upturned table of crags, had a full-frontal image that was hard not to recognize. It had been superimposed upon everything to represent lunar landings to forgotten Australian outposts. The ranch, on the other hand, had also stood in for distant planets and far frontiers, but having many more facets and dimensions made it difficult to catalogue at a glance.

This explanation elicited a smile from the inspection party, Tom included.

I escorted the scouting crew up to the Mexican hotel, which we took by foot. I maintained a respectable distance to give them the space to discuss matters in private, but Tom would not have me straggling behind. He asked that I keep near. There were questions that came to mind, and he wanted immediate answers from me. He asked what other actors had tread this set. I reported Nick Nolte, Powers Boothe, Maria Conchita Alonso, George Kennedy, and Karen Black were among his peers who had filmed here. This seemed to put him at ease.

I stood ten feet away, but whenever I heard my name, I edged next to Tom and gave my response. Then I receded to the rear of the formation until my expertise was called on again.

"Rene, can we move that wall?" Tom asked.

Bingo, I was right there to say, "Absolutely."

"You've got twenty vehicles down there in the parking lot, and we're doing a shot down here. Rene, can we move those?" He was pointing in the direction of my prop vehicle collection.

"Yeah, no problem," I affirmed.

"How long will it take?"

"One hour," I responded. "They'll be moved before you get here."

I did not wait until the last minute to do all this in case of a problem, for instance, if I could not get the semi running or I could not get the tow for the airplane. I did not want them to be grumbling, "Veluzat. We're waiting on Veluzat again." I wanted them to go and do their shot and say it was nice. It should be, "Veluzat took care of it. It's already done."

Because I was in charge of building this entire ranch, with my background as a general contractor, and because I have a penchant for achieving and acquiring licenses and different occupations,

I could provide a great many services. For example, I could look at a wall and tell you how long it would take to move it and everything else it entailed. Perhaps that was why the ranch had been such a success because I was on the job with these people, and when they asked me a question, it would not take me an hour to figure something out. They did not have to call the main office and ask someone else if they could move the wall. Most likely the construction supervisor would ask me if I would move the wall before they set up shop. They knew I built it, so I knew the best way to take it down. It would save them the trouble of doing it themselves.

This was something that I charge for, of course. They wanted it done, and I wanted the extra money. I could use the extra money to fly airplanes, helicopters, a mad money kind of thing, boy toys and such.

I would not say, "Let me think about it." It would be an immediate yes or no. I never hesitated. And I would not say like a wimp, "I don't think so." I would tell them, "The wall can be moved."

I say yes because it is positive, and my philosophy is, "We're here to make movies. We're not here to say no. We want you to do your movie."

I've always thought positive. My mother always told me, "There's nothing you cannot achieve if you set out to do it."

I have learned a little something from everyone I have worked with and tried to emulate those I have admired. Tom Cruise included. I noticed that his mannerisms were very smart; he had an intelligence about him. He held himself in a very professional fashion. He was above the temperament of a fawned-upon star. There were no screwy or insulting lapses. He was kind to everyone, but in a firm way. It was a revelation to see that he had embodied the heroic ideals that he had portrayed on screen: the pilot, the race car driver, the military attorney, the Vietnam soldier. In his manifestation as a director, which anyone could tell you was as near to deification you could get in show business, he was absolutely consummate.

When lunch was served out of the van that arrived earlier, I was invited to join them. I politely declined their offer as I always do during all strategy meetings. If this had been a shoot day and Tom Cruise had asked me to dine at his table, then I would have gladly joined their repast. But I knew they were planning their approach, time, money, people, telling secrets possibly. I was not involved with those schemes, so I separated myself. I told them that I had brought my lunch just in case we were delayed.

They asked where they should eat. I suggested in the level and cleared area next to the town, under the five-hundred-year-old oak. This venerable oak had been smacked a few times by unmindful truck drivers, seen combat action in a few fight scenes, but on that day, it was the shade for Tom Cruise's alfresco luncheon. I was asked if I had any tables or chairs. I did, but I had not anticipated them asking for them. So I had to drag them out of storage and clean them up a bit of dirt and stray insects.

I knew well enough that when people came out for their text scouts and see the Mexican town, they would become instantly smitten and begin to embroider further ideas on their new findings. They would usually use more time than they had originally allotted, and then lunchtime would roll around. I did not reproach myself for this oversight. After all, you could not be ahead of everybody.

However, there was another kind of business lunch where I would join a star. Tom Cruise and his people had said that they had not intended to stay at the ranch that long. In fact, they were on their way to another location, but they preferred to have a walking lunch here. An hour after Tom Cruise's company left, I saw a maroon Pontiac Firebird come onto the lot. It was Lorenzo Lamas. He was slated to direct and star in a show, *CIA Part II: Target Alexa*, with his then wife Kathleen Kinmont. They had done the text scout and were already in preproduction, and Lorenzo and I had numerous meetings during those processes. He extended a lunch to me because he needed me further to help him plan his maneuvers.

I assumed that Lorenzo liked me because I was a ubiquitous presence on those scouts, able to get things he needed or tell him where they could be foraged on the spot. That afternoon, I helped him fine-tune his future moves. In his work, Lorenzo required a great deal of dirt for his stunts. I availed him the use of myself and my tractor and made him dirt ramps to tip over his speeding cars. He inquired if I warehoused old tires that he might use to block out certain unnecessary views. I arranged their delivery. Later, while he was filming, he needed a flat tire inflated. He knew to come to me for the repair. It became discernible to whoever worked here at the ranch that I would try to overcome their problem so they would not have to backtrack into town. My personal service was what I was known for. Talking to Lorenzo was a pleasant way to take a meal, and we accomplished a lot.

This was the wilderness. My nearest neighbor was two miles up the road. I shared a northern boundary with the Angeles National Forest. The snakes, including the rattlesnake, deer, bears, cougars, lynx, coyotes, foxes, and other predators made life interesting around here. These were movie sets, not hermetically sealed vaults. Things ambled in; things slithered in. Things crawled in and stood their ground. Snakes, which were especially limber and determined, had scrambled through vents, clambered up roofs, and scaled trees to find comfort in our cool confines.

One day I entered the tiled lavatory that was installed on the set. I was surprise to find it already occupied by a very big rattlesnake. Even in my fright, I was able to count his seven impressive rattles. He was coiled in the corner, near the toilet. I surmised he had liberally refreshed himself with the water within and was just enjoying a break from the rigors of being a venomous hunter. Upon seeing me, he shook his tail with menace. I did not have to be aurally warned. I bounded away instinctively, keeping a protective distance between us.

When Tom Cruise was ready to leave on his helicopter, I began to panic. I knew I wanted to get a picture of him. I could already imagine the clean edge of his jaw, that world-famous smile blown up within an eight-inch-by-ten-inch frame. It would be the highlight of my burgeoning celebrity photo collection. I had sought the pictures of other actors who had visited my sets. In fact, it was becoming a reflexive solicitation to ask that they pose for me. But asking this of Tom Cruise was a much more serious endeavor. I sized up the protective cluster that surrounded and buffeted him and assessed my chances. It was a favor I particularly wanted to obtain.

This would not have occurred to me in my early days in show business. After a shot ended, I would go to my dressing room, my schoolroom, or go play with the group of other kids as I was instructed. Correlatively, the star would retire to his or her personal quarters as the routine went. I saw nothing amiss with this segregation. I did not particularly seek the company of adult actors.

Outside of the pantheon of cowboy stars, no matter how bright their name appeared on the marquees, actors were just fellow craftspeople to me.

Pictures were staged by the publicity department, a specialized skill made by a guild I had no alliance in. If I had then asked Tom to take a picture with me, it would be as unseemly as entreating him to let me direct his next picture.

I did not realize how sentimental I would become. Raymond Burr had no special place for me as a youngster. He was just another grown-up on the set. And yet how could anyone forget that baritone in the profound service of dialogue? It frightened me, and I was glad to be beyond its reach. And now that I was past the age when we first met, I had found my respect for him. I would have liked a picture of him to mark the days when I realized how a mere voice had all the suggestibility of colossal authority.

When I worked as a young tough on a television drama, I never dreamed that I was playing a scene with a future president of the United States. The image of the two of us dueling across a desk was as fixed in my mind as any photograph. If I would have known the seat of power that he was destined to occupy, I would have doled out my juvenile wiles on Ronald Reagan, to make him notice me. I would have transformed myself from the arrogant punk to a condescending supplicant as soon as the director yelled "Cut!" in order to have a joint snapshot of us. After all, I was an actor, and our glamour partly resided with those we share the lens with.

How I laugh whenever I come across myself on those Elvis Presley marathons that invariably come on his birthday. In my current portly shape, it would be hard to imagine me as one of his dancers, but I was. We were supposed to be wild, zealous, sex-driven, and intractably counter establishment—attenuated strains of the king. With our short cut hair, our fitted clothes, and those mawkish ballads we jived to, we came across as sweet and insipidly foolish instead. When I knew him during those mass-manufactured musicals, Elvis was just a beautiful doll, warbling songs and reciting lines created by committee, constructs riffing on the theory of Elvis Presley. He had fluffed off his hard edge, the collective angst of his generation, and the dervish possession that had distinguished him, leaving the carapace of a coddled and idiosyncratic idol. Elvis's resident demon of his darker younger years was successfully pushed under. It only arose during those unanticipated tantrums that no one understood. All those times we were instructed to dance and clown around him, he stared through us, like a dreamer with his eyes reluctantly open.

If I had asked a picture with Elvis Presley, I knew decisively that he would have had me thrown off the set. It was just the protocol. It was close to sedition. Unauthorized pictures were frequently sold to the press to reveal secret movie story lines or embellish a strain of ambiguous gossip. It was also considered a damn nuisance. And Elvis was not beyond strong arm tactics. So loyal partisan that I was, I never took a snapshot. Actually, it never occurred to me. I never even went through the conventional channels and sought an autographed picture of him through his publicity mill. Only the moment mattered. At that age, decline and death were merely rumors.

But recently, I have acquired a taste for memorabilia photography. I have since become more involved in the business end of show business. Stars functions were evolving. Actors had turned to directing and producing, and they were talking to people like me as equals—vendors who own the locations. This time it was they who asked for my contribution and association. They wanted to know how the ranch worked, how they could prepare their shots, how they could incorporate the land into their vision. They would appeal to me to give them reassurance. And I did. My many achievements had been tallied before. Experience counted. If my guidance was sought, invariably success would follow.

Still, the megastatus of Tom Cruise considerably dismayed me. His wattage dimmed all others. I knew from the popular press how he had been pursued heartlessly by the masses who craved him. Unfortunately, this kind of celebrity inflicts fanatic harassment even with body personnel in active defense. He was rightfully indignant that his privacy was breached repeatedly. And I who had spent the morning exchanging badinage with him, recounting funny stories of fallen stuntmen, genuinely began to like Tom Cruise as a person. A suit for his picture began to feel like an imposition. I gauged my chances for this coup as tenuous.

However, no one had ever turned down my entreaty for a picture before. Throughout the day, as Tom drafted his program, I had been assessing the right moment to make my plea. I kept my trusty little camera at the ready, just in case I sensed an opening. But those production meetings, no matter how levity prevailed, were discussions of serious import. I could not interrupt their tactical planning projections for a cheesy photograph. Shaken from my reverie, I noticed someone saying, "Okay, we're leaving." And Tom was already at the helicopter pad. At that moment, I envisioned the reality of my forthcoming failure.

There were two guys hoisting their bags into the back seat. The pilot was making a final check on the helicopter. Tom was finishing a conversation with two others. I was near them, beside the cab, the sound of the engine and the rotary blades deafening in my ears. The dust, pristine of any extraneous rubble, lifted through the air. My surroundings blurred as through a mirage while I made my last contact with him.

Tom turned to me and said, "Yes, Rene?"

"It's been a pleasure," I returned. "It is going to work out. Thank you for coming." I hesitated. I saw those around me anxious for me to complete my closing ceremony. I noticed them pulling long faces as I prolonged the moment. Suddenly, the small camera I had strapped to my side seemed very obtrusive.

Tom seemed to sense there was more to my final farewells.

"Yes, Rene?" he repeated.

I blurted out, "Tom, can I get a picture of you?" There, it was done. I had nothing to lose.

He looked me straight in the face and said, "Rene, I don't think so."

I could feel the burn of disapproval from the entourage. Their faces registered smugness and open amusement at Tom's repudiation of me. Immediately it came to me all that I had read and heard about him—that he runs from photographers. I was as guilty of badgering him as any long-lensed spy. I thought, *I am doing my job, and I love this business. What else can I do?* I liked it so much to be with these stars and to please them and to make it work. This denial meant that I had performed beneath satisfaction. Tom Cruise had vetoed my appeal. His refusal shattered me. I could not believe how his refusal would go to the heart of my self-esteem.

Then he said, "Smile, Rene."

How? I could barely manage not to crumble. I backed up one foot.

He continued, "Unless you're in it with me."

What a reversal. I had not anticipated this counteroffer. The crushing gloom evaporated. I was elated and not a little cocky that I had miffed the crowd.

He pointed out one in the assembly to take my camera. "You. Take our picture," he commanded. "Rene, give me the camera." I handed it to him automatically. The imperious general was in full effect.

Through this, I had managed to disguise my nervousness. I was as cool as they came, though inside I was quite agitated. When the camera was in the set position, like the diplomatic star that he was, Tom turned his side to the camera, faced me, and shook my hand. I responded with an equal assurance and gave him a handshake back. I prayed quickly that there were not any mechanical failures and that the film preserved the image.

After the shutter clicked, I engulfed Tom in another handshake.

"Thanks, Tom." I must have gushed. "Thanks a million. I really appreciate that."

He sized me up correctly and responded, "I know you do."

He got back into the helicopter and left. When he returned, as I previously reported, he secured all the shots that he sought and was amply pleased with the results.

The picture hung in my office gallery. It registered my moment of release and the generosity of Tom Cruise's celebrity. Although it was a handsome likeness of the two of us, I prized it more for the accompanying story. I would tell it in long and short versions on sets, while snacking at the craft service table, at Junior Chamber of Commerce meetings, in between stiff drinks. I would mention how I met Tom Cruise because any story with Tom Cruise in it would get attention. I would whip the story out anywhere, and there was rarely the photograph to illustrate it. It was as if the once coveted picture never really mattered after all.

Rene Veluzat and Tom Cruise

CHAPTER 2

Jamaican Delirium

I WAS IN that bed again. A different bed. A different life to remember. Thoughts like that would come to me when I was the most secure. When I saw bright fruit heavy on the branch or when I smelled green wood burning under a blazing sky, I was back…

With the door open to the wide veranda, eyes still shut against the Caribbean dawn, I listened to the sounds of Frenchman's Cove at its morning tasks—the gardener with his bamboo rake gathering the petals of spent flowers across the broad lawn, straw brooms in the lobby scraping against the tile in futile battle against the dust, the rolling gait of the chambermaids going from door to unlocked door. Beyond the hotel's compounds were the unsettling noises, the slashing sound of long machetes, the fall of immense vines, the brash and discordant birdsong escaping from the tight weave of the jungle. And in the quiet distance was the ocean heaving gently.

My sense of smell was still keen to those exotic days. I could easily detect the scent of the tropical sun evaporating the dew off the cool plaster in the arcade, of the cold stream, in my clean laundry, beaten daily on the rocks, of the decay in the underbrush, at once sweet and musky, and always a little, of mildew in the crease of the curtains and cushions and maybe in the close places on me.

My body was lighter; my taste buds changed. I was unused to the torpor that went on forever. I could feel the humidity already on my skin like a viscous cream, the weight of concentrated heat slowing my movements and dulling my mind. There were breezes going through my room, filtered through the treetops, steady as a great animal breathing. Already I detected the barometric change that would bring rain, torrents that would come and go like a quick temper.

The most acute feeling was the tightening around my heart that wouldn't go away. Even surrounded by my mates at work or when sleep was my direst need, I couldn't forget her. I wished for her every time I tipped my glass. I grew worse from this need. It was what I mentioned least when I told this story, but it was what I remembered the most.

In this town, they called anything related to entertainment "the industry." This was well put because people in the entertainment industry were very industrious. The greatest gift was the gift of work. In this case, a task well done was not forgotten. Years later, I received this appreciation in the form of a challenging job, so when he said Jamaica, I jumped.

It began on the ranch, two miles into the canyon at the end, on the side of the hill. I was not a man who looked upon the earth with sentimental eyes. I saw level land and remembered crops of corn and watermelon and the traversing of light trucks heavy with equipment, never aware that the actual sediment might be a somnolent soul suffering beneath its brittle crust. Because movies were so much flailing action and flexing hardware, I had a headily tallied the possibilities of every dimpled depression and nubby rise as an accessory to such certain mayhem. This hill, at the end of a canyon, would do for a ramp. I called it Turnover Canyon.

First there was a long stretch of road. It could be the roasting soils of Georgia, the black treacle that lines the way to Khartoum, the road beneath the creased and bulging clouds of the Chilean Andes, a dirt road pounded rhythmically by GI boots. It was a road because vegetation was not allowed to lie there. Otherwise, it was constructed only as a path to get to the natural ramp. Its sole design was that it was lengthy enough for a car to reach seventy-five to eighty miles an hour. At speeds that fast, a vehicle could easily turn over. Speed was necessary for such acrobatic maneuvers as flipping over a car.

And so this natural ramp looked like any ordinary hill, except it was steep. The slope was an awe-inspiring one to one. As a child, I launched myself on a cardboard sleigh down its severe sides, thrust downward in dizzying velocity, until I hit the brutal ground. Many times I would hit my jubilant head, which lead me to stare dumbly at the dark denim sky—a sure state that signified a great ride, a perfect catapult.

To get a car sufficiently launched, I would advise the stunt team to feather a tiny bank first, that is, lay down some dirt about a foot tall down to zero. This served as an intermediate slope. Thus, this temporary loamy ramp would usher the car to the greater hill that provided the immovable barrier from which hurrying cars could be properly upended. To see a car in flight, flipping like an airborne sperm whale, away from the grasp of gravity, its metallic sheen caught in the radiance of the sun, was a glorious sight.

Once the car hit terra firma, it would either keep rolling or skidding, making the alarming sound of crackling steel and ignited rubber. After the silent ascent of the floating car, a mighty crash, or reenergized screech, was a balancing release. In movies, a car in turmoil was as obligatory as a romantic kiss.

It happened thirty years ago that a stuntman, Dan Bradley, also known now as Big Dan Bradley, came to my ranch to do such a trick. I could tell by his obvious youth that he was probably twenty-five at the time and, with the darkening stains under his arms, the slick sheen on his face, that this was probably his first stunt of this kind.

I was managing the ranch at the time, toting around my water truck for wet downs and possible fires. He stood there looking at the car, as though if he peered long enough at it, instructions would miraculously be emblazoned across its sides. I asked him how he planned to roll the car over. After he told me, I warned him that it would not work very well for him. He might get hurt.

I assisted in adding extra belts to tighten the embrace of safety and informed him the best way to run up on the hill, to get the proper momentum to flip the car without flipping it before the actual placement of the stunt. Any misjudgment would have ruinous effect. Smacking the side of the hill was a sudden and hard landing.

Because this was a low-budget show. Big Dan was coordinating himself, working as stunt coordinator and stuntman. The only other person to confer with was the fire safety officer. After hearing the steps of the choreography, the fire safety officer added this amendment: that we prepare the car with only one gallon of gas in the fuel cell so as to prevent excess gas spilling along the road. The danger being that the metal of the car could hit a rock while skidding, causing a spark, inflaming the car with superfluous fuel, causing it to blow up with the driver helplessly cinched and lashed down.

To prepare, we gathered all the rocks and unnecessary rubble from the mile-long road. I released a spray of water from my truck to damped the dust into manageable dirt. I helped Dan bind himself with the safety harness, the thick safety belts that were bolted to the floor with hook eyes from underneath the car to the top of the floorboard. There was such cross leverage to the waist and cross leverage to the chest that it sucked him back into the seat. Beside him was the rip cord, a cord that he would use to pull himself over to the safety of the passenger side so that when debris and trees went flying through the windshield, he could keep himself low until all harm had passed overhead and out the back window.

The stunt began with the powerful acceleration of the car across that nameless, featureless road. The mound of soil held long enough to pitch the car upward, where the hill was waiting to sling it momentarily aloft. The car held like a cumbersome and weighty projectile until it was called duly to the ground, where it rolled over and over in the excitable dirt. The car shed its skin in a very becoming manner, tossing off plates of steel and plastic accessories. Dan came out of the car safe, to the sound of earned applause, all his moving parts still attached.

His first words to me, leveled at my eyes, were, "Rene, I owe you one!"

My modest response in the exhilaration of the moment was, "Dan, you don't owe me nothin'. I'm just happy to see you."

When it was over, I never thought of the stunt or Dan again. Never saw the film the stunt ran in. If the stunt had gone bad, I would have felt bad every time I went up that canyon. As it was, success created its own oblivion.

Ten years passed. Big Dan called me, and I remembered him and the stunt. Scores had hurled themselves off Turnaround Canyon since, each taking that temporary flight without incident, without further remark. But Big Dan wanted to repay me back for an imaginary debt. To work in rigging three Jeeps for Denzel Washington was what he offered, a three-day gig overseas. It was what I based my behavior on—that each of my good turns might someday be rewarded with another. In this case, the placement was Jamaica.

My job was to equip the Jeeps with special brakes and racing steering. Army Jeeps were ordinarily lumbering creatures, developed for their traction and determination on rough roads. Steering a Jeep was like coaxing an ungainly elephant. When urged to come to an immediate stop, they performed their task in due course, halting eventually. But the Jeeps for this movie were meant to be hybrid ballerinas, able to turn swiftly in tight circles with only the slightest nudge. Imagine a bull male in full charge asked to do a pirouette en pointe at the slightest provocation.

Big Dan asked me to name my price, and I did. He gave me the terms I asked for and a driver for my personal use. I could not help but feel a gingery anticipation as I prerigged the Jeeps at the ranch. It was at the end of summer. I boxed everything into crates, taped them up, and packed what I needed for what I thought would only be a three-day enterprise on a paradisiacal isle.

I had never been in Jamaica before. I didn't expect a Hawaiian-style lei greeting and kiss, but I surely did think I would be subjected to a strip search either.

The tools I brought to cover any event included connecting cables, gurneys, clamps, wire, tie wire, bolts, nuts, screws, and then all the stuff to make them work. I carried straps and all kinds of rigging for anything I might need and then the Sagnoff racing string, which looked like long pipes.

My first impression of Jamaica was convention oven–like heat, a small room, and a big woman guard with plying fingers. Customs hustled me off the plane at arrival because they induced the pipes for the Sagnoff steering were to make guns. All day they interrogated me, suspicious that I was trafficking in illegal gun manufacturing. They even searched for further evidence of munition parts.

Finally, the studio vouched for my supplies, and I was set free. The box I had packed my gear in was shredded, and so was my mind.

I spent the night in Kingston, but it was not a restful one. I heard the sound of machine guns firing and airplanes dive bombing. Understandably I thought we were under attack. I jumped out of my bed and ran to the concierge. He assured me it was nothing more than gun runners and dope peddlers being picked out of the sky.

"Yeah, mon," he said with the nonchalance of repeating the explanation every day to skittish tourist. "They're just shooting down a dope plane."

The next day, it took an hour and a half for my driver to make the trip from the airport at Kingstown to Port Antonio. The single-lane roads were a capricious mix of asphalt and dirt, frequently frosted over by mud that slithered down from the adjoining hills. Breeches and deeply scooped pits, as well as bulges in disturbing series and spot rises, embellished the surface. The entire course seemed to be the effect of careless excavation. I could not hold my seat; it was not unlike being caught in a difficult trot.

The weather leaped to extremes. One moment the powerful sun would be extracting every bit of moisture from my body, and I would weep sweat from every pore. When the rain came, it cut the sun to a quick, splicing in a determined squall. It was a clamorous and effusive downpour. My driver, blinded by the silver shower, did well by seeking out the safety of the road's shoulder. Inside, while we waited, I felt the pressure of the rain jostling the frame of the car. Five minutes later, when the sun took over again, its character was equally as ferocious, simmering me in my very blood.

There were a few cars in the vicinity en route to my hotel. But there were people in their curious costumes. The men wore little bits of cloth around their loins, maybe more so as a fashion expression rather than for modesty's sake, for their clothes were in such tatters only the ruins remained. Perhaps the constant weather swings had hastened their decay. Each man completed his scanty attire with a big gleaming machete. As we passed them, they held them aloft by great chiseled arms. They brandished these sharpened tools, grinning in greeting or grimacing in warning.

The women had their midsections as perilously contained as the men. Because car travel was so slow, I was able to observe at leisure the rolling globes of their buttocks; I got close enough to see the effects of humidity between their passing cheeks. Around their breast, they wore tight bandeau tops that hardly did the job of concealment. They favored vivid colors that were so complementary against ebony skin.

The women's most striking accessory was a head laden with goods—piles of shopping or commerce. What equilibrium and posture these women possessed to carry burdens that spanned to cover the weight of firewood to the frailty of eggs stacked into confident towers on their heads! If that wasn't enough, the women's cargo also included balancing children on either hip. I saw them place breast into hungry mouths. At the roadsides, they supported the arms of squatting toddlers. Hands that were free were used to gesture in conversation to a neighbor, whole arms flying for further articulation.

People wove in and out of the verdant landscape. It was an environment so dense that after a few steps into the bright green folds of the jungle, a person would appear swallowed whole or come forth unexpectedly through tiny rents. They cut niches with machetes, making long tunnels through which they made their way. The sounds of severing could be heard as regular as beating birds in the underbrush.

The travelers on the road loped along in a slow, steady pace, their plodding steps a means of conserving energy. A measured walk was a suitable adaptation in incessant heat. They also paused as we did, on the side of the road, when storms made their movement unstable.

From what I could see during my journey, the houses they lived in were virtual shacks. Their sides were no more than unsubstantial cardboard, and the roofs were made of corrugated tin or palm leaf. At ten feet by ten feet, my rented car was nearly as roomy as their floorless shelters. They must have utilized them only for sleep though, because whole families seemed to be quite settled in the yard, washing their hair, grinding spices, dancing to an internal percussion.

All around us the jungle grew in bursting good health. Tree trunks had barely enough room to sway in the ruffling winds. Plants of every order competed in open hostility for each bit of ground. Mid-level leaves opened expansively to slurp in the sun, the constant arrival of rain. The air was left for the clutches of tortuous vines. On the ground, the rapacious creepers stole around shallow roots. Flowers and fruits fell from their perches, spreading their genes for the next generation.

Jamaica can boast fertile plains that make agriculture a basic industry. But it is a land whose emerging summits make the most lasting impression. The island is what remains of the third largest tip of an ancient mountain range that submerged into the sea and then rose again to form the West Indies. The road to my hotel barely threaded the fractured mountainsides, those peaks that ascended past the cloud of water. Cliffs broke away into deep gorges. Headlands stood against the sea. Streams foamed from rainy runoff, small ones, large ones, none of them navigable for anything but the smallest crafts and simplest rafts. Waterfalls tumbled from the sheer summits, noisy and rainbow-ridden. They even refreshed the waders fishing on the transparent reef.

I floated through a veil of cinnamon, allspice, and nutmeg. I added myself to the setting with my own special flavor, peeing into various watercourses from exalted heights.

Along the coast, on the road that would eventually lead to San Antonio, we left the Blue Mountain range whose steep walls prompted the rain clouds to rupture. We were still made wet, however, by the long arm of sea sprays, splashing us through the open window—my first taste of the Caribbean smacked of salt.

I arrived at my hotel and looked back at the rocky bluffs, the running blue of unruly streams, the braided cushion of the jungle and saw that even distance could not soften the mountains' craggy drama. Frenchman's Cove, near the northeast corner of the island, a resort borne of Canadian investment, was barely shelter from all that rampant wilderness.

If the jungle could strangle human compounds, I was sure it would. By day, I saw it expanding like a multicelled organism. As night fell, the dark panting mass might have been invisible, but it remained frightfully palpable.

The hotel itself was a one-building affair, white with open verandas. It was a '60s interpretation of a French plantation. The millionaire who developed it had a motto, "Hang the expense!" It was a sentiment I have found often repeated in the movie industry as well.

Within the grounds, order reigned. The hotel glimmered in aristocratic splendor, aloof from the overwrought jungle. Walls were smooth, metal polished, and floors and roofs proved sound. Vigilant gardeners kept the lawns clipped to military precision. When the limber palms shed their fronds, they were whisked away before they littered the tidy paths. Bedding plants led the eye to open views. One could sit at breakfast and have no barrier from the sound of banana leaves shredding in the trade winds, the bright birds landing on the balustrade to peck at unseen crumbs. And yet one felt safe from nature's reach.

The spot was chosen because of the celebrated cove. It was a landlocked arm of the sea. The water in the cove was so intensely blue painters had yet to reproduce the color correctly. It was mysteriously deep and unbelievably clear. At certain times of the day, the water had a purple cast to it, and where it was rimmed by trees, green shadows lay across its sleepy shores. To lie upon its white sand beaches was to fall upon a sleeve of silk.

The price for this idyll was high. I paid fifty dollars for a hamburger. It was imported. We had no ice. No ice. So I drank beverages that grew tepid in the fixed heat. My diet consisted of tropical fruits—bananas, grapefruits, oranges, watermelons. But they did not taste like the ones I was familiar with; they were more tart than sweet, and there were instances when the flavor seemed to be a cross between two fruits, a watermelon mixed with grapefruit, for example. Then again, grapefruits were at once sweeter and tart at the same time. Because my diet was soon to resemble one a Silverback gorilla might choose, I had plenty of opportunity to savor these peculiar combinations.

In those days, my drink was whiskey. The first time I ordered it from the barman, I was stunned.

"Wow! What the hell is this?" I bellowed after taking a sip.

"Ya mon, that's whiskey," he answered in all innocence.

I reached over to his station. "Let me see the bottle," I demanded. It said Scotch whiskey. They mixed Scotch and whiskey together and came up with that.

Everything there was a little different. Every day was really strange.

I only took enough clothes for three days, and I ended up staying thirty days. Those clothes became sorry specimens. Each night as I took my shower, the clothes disappeared. Washerwomen would come into my room and take them to the rushing streams and beat them of the scent and stain of toil. They provided this service without asking, lingering in the doorway afterward, leaving me with only a towel around my waist for dignity, while they hinted of diversions we could enjoy as my clothes dried.

During the day, I did my job for the studio, and while we were filming, there would be hundreds of these native people watching us. They must have heard on the coconut wireless where we would be, because no matter where we set up, there they were, a cast of thousands, waiting in the wings. At night, the crew would go back to the hotels in cars and vans and trucks. This was the moment the hangers-on made their move. As our convoy drove out, the locals streamed behind us, running to keep apace.

They started en masse, legions of sleek-skinned natives, pumping their legs and arms along the return route. As this was a long journey and the vehicles more powerful and faster than even the swiftest runner, only few survived the hour-long trip. The ones who did complete the race followed us to our rooms. I ran to mine each night, the hot breath of my pursuer upon my back.

Once inside, I held the door with the of weight of my body, not sure that the frail locks would hold. On the other side came the offer of sweet enticements.

"Let me rub your hands," a voice cooed.

"My hands are fine," I retorted.

"I will massage you. Make you feel relaxed."

"I don't need a massage," I answered wearily.

"I'm going to make love to you," the high voice insisted.

"No, you're not!" I shouted back, panicked. "Leave me the hell alone!"

I declined every act of physical attention. We were warned about excruciating and horrifying sexually communicable diseases. I worried about my health and my reputation among my peers. I could not bring disgrace and harm back to my wife.

But still the women appeared—old crones, young matrons with children to suckle, shy coquettes, and brazen hussies. They opened up the shower door and knelt at my bedside. In the moonlight, I could see their dark areolas through the gauzy white material of their tight apparel. With their gestures, they spoke of pleasure, lips bitten, hips waving, the light brushing of fingers against erect nipples.

In the heat, their bodies seemed like cool oases, and I was a man who needed to be cooled. I admit that I wished the obstacles of fidelity and health could be dismissed. Each woman who fixed me with her smoldering eyes tested my resolution. When I was finally left alone, I contemplated the scent that lingered, the texture of dusky skin almost captured in my hand.

The threat of sex was all around us. When we went to bars, we went in the safety of groups. The most common scenario posed was someone would slip you a Mickey into your drink, steal your money, and screw your brains out, leaving you hurt, penniless, and ridden with a sexually transmitted disease. It was a testament to our wholesome resolve that none of us left the island harmed.

Out of paranoia, I kept my hands covered with gloves. When I worked on the Jeep, I wore thin cotton gloves that protected my skin from cuts and abrasions. By the end of the day, they would be ripped and gouged. I figured it was easier to replace the gloves than leave myself vulnerable to disease or infection that I feared was carried by wind or casual contact. During the course of my days off, I switched to rubber gloves, ever suspicious of every doorknob and bathroom fixture.

The stuntman who doubled Denzel Washington was an African American man from Valencia, one of the towns in the valley I live in. He came to me, briefing me on the depth of the crag the stunt was to be executed near. If he fell, he would tumble five hundred to one thousand feet to tire boulders and river below. As it frequently happens in making movies, the initial plan was scraped for a newer, more energized version. He was afraid of sacrificing his life for a moment of celluloid pandemonium.

Since Denzel Washington deserved more than a Putt-Putt near car crash, it was decided that the speed of the traveling vehicles would be accelerated, the collision to be one of infinite closeness, and a 180-degree turn to be performed at the perilous edge of the ledge. The problem lay in the crumbly composition of the road. There was loose dirt and an uneven layer of rock in which to slide upon uncontrollably. Cinematically, spraying debris added to the excitement of an action shot, but it was ungovernable and, in this case, could lead to headlong death.

Big Dan Bradley, as coordinator, conferred with me on the obstacles. I recommended the only way the job was to be done safely was to cable the Jeep. He did not care about the cost or the mechanics of the situation, only that it be done.

"Do it," Big Dan said. "Fix it. Make it right."

I was given a truck in which to pick up supplies from Port Antonio. I brought back one thousand feet of cable from the docks. Then with the ton of tools I brought and the hooks and eyes I had purchased, I equipped the Jeep with the steel cable, a tether I hoped would hold.

I explained to the stuntman that if the Jeep was going to go over the cliff, the vehicle would most likely be safe, but I could not vouch for him.

"If you do go off, you're gonna hang," I said.

"Well, my god, what happens if I'm hanging over the cliff?" he asked.

"If you're not strapped in, you're gonna fall out and die. You're gonna die anyway, only the Jeep is gonna hang. You're not."

The stuntman took my fair warning and rigged his own special harness to tie himself in securely. It was for him to do, not me. It was his life, his job. He did, however, approve the modifications I had made to the Jeep and the eyelet running over the bumper to the one thousand feet of cable.

My job was to install the brakes and the Saginaw racing steering. Sagnofif racing steering has special properties other than its substitutability for the barrel of a gun. They are a special steering column wheel bearings that make the steering wheel turn very fast and respond just as rapidly. It is also called positive steering. This setup allows you to maneuver the steering wheel and have the tires quickly follow. Whereas in Jeeps, when you give the steering wheel a half turn, the tires are just warming to the suggestion. This Jeep rotated immediately without hesitation. I fixed the brakes for hyperperformance as well. By tapping the brakes, the stop became violently sudden. You could stop on a dime and get nine cents change.

The scene in the movie had Denzel Washington as the chief of police coming around the bend of a mountain road. In the opposite direction, Robert Townsend, as his good friend, who was also a character of shady dealings, drove a motorcycle and sidecar hell-bent for leather. Because each vision was obscured by the hairpin turns, in a heated dramatic moment, their vehicles came upon each other and almost collided head-on. Instead, at the last possible instant, Washington drove his Jeep expertly out of harm's way, braking abruptly, averting disaster, but coming out of his spin at the slick edge of the precipice.

When the director shouted "Cut!" we told the stuntman to stay seated. It was a near miss. The back tires practically floated over the rushing water of the deep ravine. All hands grabbed the front of the Jeep to stabilize it while we pulled him up. After we made a fuss over him and gave each other self-congratulatory pats on the back, I reveled in the moment then set my course on going home.

"Oh no, you're not. You're not going home," Big Dan Bradley told me.

"What do you mean, Dan?" I inquired.

"Hey, you can't leave now. I've got other stunts and things to do. And when I saw what you did here, we need you for the rest of the show."

"No. I gotta go home."

"We're gonna make it worth your while. You gotta stay."

So I figured what the hell. Might as well. That was how a three-day stay became a month shanghaied.

While I was there, the other two Jeeps had broken down. I ordered the parts from the mainland and set up shop under the protection of the banana trees. I laid out all the car parts and my tools on the ground, spread them on thick banana leaves as big as coffee tables, which I cut fresh every morning. When it rained, I huddled close to the stem of the plant, prying apart a piece of fruit and eating it while I waited.

The Jeeps were a character in the movie. I was asked to modify them to execute stops and turns they were not designed to do. For example, when you put your foot on the brake, ordinarily all four brakes would stop, or you would make a big circle and go the other way eventually. That would make for a very boring chase scene. Under my tampering, I customized the Jeeps where you pulled one handle, which was an extra pair of brakes, that only locked up one of the back wheels or both back wheels or whatever was wanted. Then you turned the front of the car or the racing steering that turned it. You locked the brakes up, and as it spun, the car would go right around in a tight circle and would go back the other way. The unreality of the situation of laying on the brakes of a Jeep so that it would spin and go back in the opposite direction right in the same spot made high-speed pursuits in the movies very exciting.

But that all came later. For the first week and a half, after my initial three days, I was told to hang out and wait. And so I did, bringing my chair out to the cove, setting it up in the shallows, wearing my swim trunks and hat to watch the world go by. Everything from the hotel was charged to the studio. At the beach, I was a self-proclaimed mogul, attended by three devoted hotel employees who fetched and carried my tumblers of rum and brought a cornucopia of fruits whenever my appetite arose. I smoked Royal Jamaica cigars until the sun set, enjoying their smooth taste mixed with the sweet and salty air of the beach, which, in itself, was its own refreshment. The girls rubbed my shoulders as the water eddied around my ankles or fallen hand, inducing me to meditate on the abundance of the universe. Later, before I left, I gathered into a blue bottle of Perrier the thin, delicate, and light sand that had intoxicated my toes.

When I did work, it was just for a day, and then I would have four days off. In the office, during downtime, I would knock back a case and half of Red Stripe beer, the local brew. In the dense heat, it came out of my body and formed a thick paste of sweat on my skin. We ate jerk chicken that the coordinator Ray would send out for. It was a delicious dish, the best thing I had eaten on the island. We crew members licked off our lips the marinade of crushed chilies, spices, and herbs, dousing the chicken repeatedly with Jamaican hot sauce that seared our tongues raw.

One day, I suggested to Ray that we eat at the restaurant where the jerk chicken was cooked instead of in the crowded office. With reluctance, he agreed. Six of us piled into a big crew cab and headed down the road. As we traveled, the roads became narrower and narrower, the jungle more pervasive. Soon the road evaporated into a thin dirt track. There were bonfires everywhere, burning sugarcane and garbage, and it brought to us the scent of unknown flesh.

We were greeted by native men outfitted with glinting steel machetes and dangling sexual apparatus. Children were siphoning milk from their mothers. The houses were huts of interlaced bamboo and tin. Upturned cars served the purpose of rusted shelters. Nothing resembled the structure of a restaurant.

Finally, Ray said, "The jig is up. The jig is up."

"What are you talking about?" I asked.

"There it is over there."

I looked to where he pointed. "What?"

Five dozen Jamaicans stood around a huge bonfire pit. Chickens ambled about freely, scratching out grubs in the dust.

"We're here," proclaimed Ray as we all got out of the womb of the truck.

"Where's this restaurant?" I insisted again.

"I just don't know what to tell you," he began. "There is no big restaurant. Here's how they eat over here."

A man who obviously recognized us as business took our order. "Ya mon," he repeated, "six jerk chickens comin' up."

And with that said, he took his machete and gouged it into the guts of the closest unfortunate chicken. Then he whacked off the chicken's head with a mighty swipe. The head rolled until it stopped by the fire drum. Using his teeth as a fine instrument, the cook proceeded to pluck the fowl clean of all its feathers and debone it as skillfully as any cordon bleu chef. Within moments, the denuded and filleted morsels were rolled in an aromatic concoction, ready to be skewered at the end of a sharpened stick.

The bird, which so recently had been alive and unconcerned for its eventual fate, was held aloft a glowing hollow, dripping from its own grease. My stomach heaved itself upward in reaction to the savage display. Somehow, though, I managed to keep myself together.

In three minutes, the chef pulled the skewered bird from the fire and presented it to me. "Ya mon, yours is ready. Yours is ready," he said, brandishing the still raw meat inches before my nose.

Ray interceded. He asked that our meals be cooked to a less bloody degree as we were unaccustomed to the habits of native cookery. The chef complied.

Ray, meanwhile, had noticed that I had taken a greenish tinge. I could not hide that I was overwhelmed by the atrocious decapitation and dismemberment. His quick medical advice was that I be brought Red Stripe beer. I quaffed it down obediently. The beverage slightly revived me.

It occurred to me the term *jerk chicken* referred to the awful death throes the poor beast suffered as it made its way reluctantly to the barbecue pit. I could not bear to eat the chicken or stay a moment longer. We left the macabre site.

Back at the office, we halted our rumbling stomachs with further applications of Red Stripe beer. Between swigs, I read the label. It said it was the original Jamaican beer, bottled in Jamaica with Jamaican water.

I thought, *Oh my god, we're not supposed to drink Jamaican water, and I've been drinking this beer for three weeks. It's in this beer.*

That night, I became sick. I was so sick I was permanently affixed to my bed. I was not alone in my infirmary. Half the crew had taken ill with various and exotic illnesses. Ordinarily, the nurse would be the one to dispense our medicine, but she was also in an indisposed state.

I lay in my bed befuddled by fever and delirium. My stomach was in turmoil. I heaved the contents of my stomach, and when it emptied, I continued to wretch repeatedly. My body convulsed with spasms that lift me from the rumpled sheets. I was so weak my head failed to turn on my sodden pillow. I was so weak the effort to blink my eyes was beyond me.

The crew and help were one hour away in Port Antonio. I felt my isolation at Frenchman's Cove most sharply as I smelled the dank jungle odor come through the open window. I wondered if I would be found decomposed and decayed like the stuff of the spongy undergrowth. I thought I was going to die, and it made me turn maudlin. I wept real tears that I was too feeble to remove. My lost family especially grieved me. The events of my life came at me thick and fast.

Then there came a knock at my door. The time was nine in the morning. It was a doctor, and he was tall, good-looking, and thin as any cinema hero, wearing black pants and white silk shirt. He went to my bedside and put his steady hand on my quivering brow.

"Ya mon," he said in his professional manner, "you've got jungle fever. You are sick bad. Real bad. But I'll fix you right up."

He had with him a black case, and from that black case, he began to mix vials together. When he was done with his impromptu brew, he placed it before me and urged me to down it completely.

I looked at the contents of the glass, and it was the vilest green. It moved in the container like sea sludge. When I sniffed it suspiciously, it stank of the most awful foul rot.

Without considering my feelings for the appalling stuff, he continued to persuade me to drink it. He was not gentle in his urgings.

"You drink this. You will be well."

"If I drink this," I countered, "I will die."

"If you don't drink this, you will die," he said darkly to me. "Ya mon, you are very sick. You are worse than anyone else."

His comparison did not please me. I had a heavy decision to make. To me it was fifty-fifty. Drink it and die, or take the chance and not drink it and 99.9 percent I would die. At that time, my math was not too good. I decided to swallow.

It was not a pleasant decoction. I held my nose to get it close enough to drink. Once I opened my mouth, it slithered down my throat like ooze from a polluted stream. To distract myself from its repulsiveness, I beat my face from side to side. I swore and gulped with alternate breaths.

The doctor did not take kindly to the dregs that remained in the glass. He sternly ordered me to drink it dry.

"All of it, mon," he commanded as I slurped it in three messy gulps. Portions of the syrup trickled down the sides of my mouth. Needless to say, I did not clean myself with my tongue or smack my lips.

Satisfied with my performance, the doctor left. "You'll be fine, mon," he said in a congratulatory way. "You'll be fine."

Fifteen minutes later, I was up and taking a shower. The studio called, and I assured them of my miraculous recovery.

Who knows how I contracted the illness? It could have been the water or through people. A simple act of close respiration near a sick soul could have been the reason I fell to the ailment. Or perhaps it was the emotional turmoil of seeing a live chicken disemboweled so ruthlessly.

It had also been suggested to me that we of the crew had been put a hex on by the local witch doctor. The movie company had chosen to film on his considered holy land, a beautiful jungle area with a little hut and a small graveyard. The witch doctor, in understandable vengeance, turned the power of his voodoo upon us.

I made the mistake of examining the hut. I was curious to see the set. It had a bamboo roof, and inside there were few furnishing like books and things set on rickety tables. I also walked on the burial grounds. There were tiny wooden crosses, maybe thirty in total.

I never heard the curse being uttered or saw the witch doctor. I was told he wore feathers in his headpiece with glitter beads. It was not unreasonable that his curse extended to me in absentia.

My drinking habits began to change. I switched from Scotch whiskey to rum and Coke. Quickly I was sipping straight rum. The island rum was the greatest. It did not need any additives or accompaniments. It was delicious enough in itself.

My days were unconstructed. I worked five hours a day, or I left immediately as my scenes were completed. Then I'd be off for a two-day rum binge. I asked for repatriation to the States repeatedly.

One day, a Jeep caught fire. The crew jumped around like clowns in a slap stick comedy, fetching buckets of water to douse out the flames. But in their panic, the crew's aim was not steady, and the buckets of water emptied onto each other instead of at the intended flame. I, in my inimitable calm, took off my shirt and beat the fire into smoldering submission. The fire had started under the dashboard, and I directed all my efforts there.

"The fire's out! The Jeep's fixed!" I shouted above the frenzied mob. "Let's go with it."

The shirt was lost to the cause, but then again, I was losing a lot of clothes anyway.

When I needed to do a bit welding on a Jeep, I used manpower instead of electricity. A man was set on a bicycle, which, in turn, was rigged to a generator with two wires. This was only steps below the Volkswagen motor, I was told, that the city of Port Antonio used as a power plant. Was it any wonder that my new, shiny Sear Craftsman tools began to dwindle? By the time my stint was over, I had two pairs of pliers left. Some tools I gave away in appreciation for the help I received. Others disappeared into the jungle's greedy grasp.

I soon developed a fine fellowship with my driver. He lived in the jungle with his family, and he frequently invited me there for a visit. He recommended the bars I should call upon and offered to introduce me to clean girls. He wore a Hawaiian-style shirt, pants, and shoes. He was a normal person and had good work habits.

Then there were others who were not as agreeable.

It was decided one day that six of us would take the drive from Port Antonio to Kingston. Our means of transportation would be the camera truck. This vehicle was a Ford truck that had been rebuilt with a flatbed on it. It came equipped with chrome and aluminum railings around it, to attach the camera, lights, reflectors, and generators. It had three platforms—on the roof of the truck, a little further down, and then a lower platform—so there were three heights to set the camera. Altogether it was a gruesome-looking thing—metal, shiny, and huge.

Apparently, camera trucks were not welcome under the jungle forest canopy. We embarked on what we thought would be a jaunty trip through the island's interior. It was not to be so. The natives, so unaccustomed to much tourist traffic through their dark woods anyway, did not fancy the look of our wheels. When we came into their view, they showed their scorn by shouting angrily at us. They used words that made no sense but, by their delivery, were meant to be bruising. They shook their muscular aims at us. Brutish-looking weaponry extended their reach. At times they chased us on foot, nearing the truck as we slowed around the many bends. They hacked at us in all seriousness and threw their machetes with fortunate inaccuracy.

We made it to Kingston town and took in the sights of the metropolis. The bustling craft markets were very stimulating after so much rustic isolation. We were impressed by the many fine municipal buildings and the array of tasty victuals in the city's charming restaurants. By night, though, we had to make the reverse trip.

It was just as harrowing. We encountered an uprising at every station and point. It was as if we had started a small war in which we were the lone and hated enemy. Again, the men, wearing no more than G-strings and faces of contempt, chased us down in a deliberate manner. Though we always ran apace of them, we could hear the fury of their blades slashing past us. Like missiles, their machetes pierced the air, landing ineffective blows on the truck's armament of chrome and aluminum. We inside were preserved by careful ducking and the shields that the truck inadvertently provided. In the end, we emerged untouched.

But it was enough for me. Even though I was needed for another couple of weeks, I asked and finally received my final withdrawal.

The problem began with transportation to the airport at Kingston. From my recent experience, I was in no mood to repeat the harassing I had received previously. They expected me to take the return route through the hostile jungle. I let them know this option would not be entertained.

They pronounced, "No problem."

I was instructed to make haste and gather my gear. A driver in a van came to pick me up. For an hour, we wandered through the dreaded jungle.

"Where the hell is this airport?" I asked indignantly.

The driver responded, "Right around the corner, mon. Right around the corner."

Sure enough, we pulled around the corner, and there was this little airport. On either side of the tiny runway, crashed airplanes lay in careless heaps. These planes had been violently brought down from the sky and lay mined beyond repair. They were the results of the government's drug intervention program.

I paid the driver and sat amid this aviation cemetery, waiting for my private chartered plane to take me to Kingston. I eased back with my two bags, hat, cigar, souvenirs, and money for the last leg of this venture. I was alone for quite a while in this clearing and spent.it noting the wreckage around me.

Finally, I heard the sound of this teeny, tiny Cessna airplane. It was not symmetrical as its American counterparts. There were dents in it. It looked quite abused. It was lopsided. Everything looked crooked to me.

The plane attempted to land but bounced a few times before it got right. It rolled to a stop, which I figured meant that it was still mechanically controlled.

Out of this demented plane came two pilots, spiffy and regulative as any officers of a 747 jet. They wore captains' hats, white starched shirts with fancy epaulets on their shoulders.

"Are you Rene Veluzat?" they inquired politely.

"Yes," I said.

"Yeah, mon, we're taking you out of here, to the big airport."

I was glad that they did not confuse my itinerary.

"You got the money with you?" I was asked.

I answered affirmatively. They let me board. Or should I say they loaded me up.

I embarked on the plane, but other than the two pilot's seats. There were no other places to sit. They offered me a box to rest on, and I took it, although I would have wished for a more conventional chair. I sat in the back, in the freight section. The exposed headliner's upholstery hung irritating in my face. Luckily, I did not need it to cling to because the maintenance crew had the forethought to install seat belts in the floor. I wrapped those belts tightly around myself as I balanced on my crate.

Take of was not an easy deed. This poor little plane grunted and groaned, trying to lift off the ground. As we eventually inclined upward, the fire extinguisher and all my loose parcels started to roll freely on the floor.

Suspiciously, we did not immediately take the route I had expected. The pilot steered toward the open ocean and started to circle. After two or three times, I asked him about his meandering course.

"Yeah, mon," he agreed with me. "We are in the ocean. We have to go this way to Kingston, to get your plane."

Kingston was in the opposite direction.

I mulled over all possible dreadful scenarios. My silence must have troubled him. "Yeah, mon," he said, placating me, "no problem."

After five minutes of this repeated circling pattern, I began to argue with his judgement.

"Yeah, mon," I said, adopting the island's expression, "you are going the wrong way."

"No problem," he said once again.

"We are supposed to go the other way," I suggested nervously.

He explained to me in his best reassuring captain's voice. "We can't go the other way. We gotta get over the hills. We have to circle in the ocean to get the altitude with this plane."

When we finally reached the altitude needed, which was about one thousand feet, he headed back toward land. The plane then advanced upon the hills. Jamaica lay beneath me—green, shielded, and varied with streams. However, we're not high enough to really soar over the loftier portions of the landscape.

"Yeah, mon," I said, pointing out the nearing terrain. "You are about to hit that tree. The wheels are too low."

Then I admitted my feelings to him, to evoke some compassion out of him.

"You are scaring me."

The rum came in very handy. I nipped steadily from its contents.

It became obvious that we had not increased our elevation. The pilot provided his own assessment. "Mon, too much weight. Too much weight, mon. We can't get the plane up."

"I'll throw out my bags," I said with my hand already on my case. "I don't care."

"No, no, don't throw out your bags" came his reply.

The wheels were already brushing the tops of the trees. There were cut branches left in our wake. I was frightened, and on my crate, I was squirming fitfully. Somehow, we managed to avoid the leas pliant mountaintops.

Then I heard the motor quitting. It was not good to hear the absolute quiet of a plane in flight. I brought this to his attention.

"The motor is dying!" I screamed. "The plane is going down."

The pilot automatically responded, "No problem, mon. No problem."

Meanwhile, he pushed buttons in a seemingly random pattern and took to jerking all the other controls that he could grasp. The two of them pounded and yanked until the plan resuscitated. As we neared an unscheduled descent, it finally did. The motor spotted on, and we went up.

The rum and I were continuously entwined. We bopped from one tree to another.

Then the pilot informed me, "Yeah, mon, we are about to land." I looked down for a cleared runway. There was nothing but the jungle.

"Hey, mon," I said, peering carefully for a break in the topography. "Where is the airport?"

The pilot answered, "No airport, mon. We land in the jungle. We got no license to fly this."

This stunning piece of news sent me back to the attention of my bottle. But I was not blind enough to witness our landing. A tiny road was spied and that was where we descended our craft. The captain and his crew were able enough, without the benefit of processing and accreditation, to fly clear of the swishing banana trees and oversized palms, and drop that broken toy of a plane neatly on the cleared ground.

I called the name of my maker in gratitude. I looked around, not really knowing what would be my next move. We were, after all, in a thick forest.

The pilot asked for his due renumeration. I scooped out of my pockets with damp hands. He pointed toward an off-shoot road.

"Yeah, mon," he said, instructing me down a dubious path, "go through the fence there. Cross the runway."

I tried to make out the fence through the jungle's foliage. "You there?" he repeated, encouragingly. "You there."

I gathered my two bags, my cane, my hat, and what was left of my life-affirming rum. I found the fence that opened to the runway. The runway crisscrossed with the airline traffic. There was nothing else I could do but walk across the lines of transit. I lumbered along, under the burden of all my things, my sights of the airport in the distance.

My tramp did not go unnoticed. I heard the terrifying squeal of a police car in pursuit. That was a signal for me to pick up the pace. I did, running as fast as I could, to avoid explaining the details of my illegal flight. I did not want to be caught and held under suspicion again.

When I made it to the other side, the cops posed the question that I had expected since I ran from his chase.

"Hey, mon, where did you come from?" he asked.

"I got in the wrong way, the wrong door," I said, mustering my best acting ability. "I've got to get inside. I'm flying out of here."

He listened to my answer and sized me up for the deranged tourist that I was. Then he let me go with this warning. "Well, don't cross that runway no more. You might have been killed."

As I paid for my ticket, I was told that I owe 10 percent more. I gave the ticket seller what I had left after having paid for porters and tips. I had not been told to budget correctly. All that remained was a measly dollar. With that dollar, I refreshed myself with a beer.

An hour passed. It was past the time of the plane's departure. I asked an airport employee the meaning of the delay.

"Ya, mon," he said. "No problem. They ate working on the plane." Then he added ominously, "The plane needs a little work." Two hours went by, and I grew hot and sticky. The beer had been drained long ago, and I was craving a replacement. Now I had become a bum. I asked a Jamaican stranger to buy me a drink because I had not thought to bring my credit card for what I thought would be a three-day job. I was left to bum for my booze. And I needed it too. There was no air conditioning. I was still pumped up from my harrowing plane flight and my near escape from the law. The studio had paid for everything, but they could not spare me this humiliation. The beer cost a quarter. I paid for it with my pride.

The announcement was made that the plane was ready. But I was diverted to a private screening room. A huge Jamaican woman wanted to inspect my private parts again. I began to tire of intimate inspections.

"Assume the position!" she barked.

"What for?" I asked irately.

"We have to check you. To see if you bring dope out of the country. You know people come here to take ganja."

"Ganja?"

"Ganja. The island word for marijuana." She made me take off my shirt but was not satisfied with just that. She instructed me to take off my pants too. Then she took inventory of the contents of my shorts and prodded me officially.

I was excruciatingly angry. My clothes were in an untidy pile, and I was dripping with sweat. "I don't got no dope," I bellowed at her. "I'm trying to get the hell off this goddamn island." This dramatic display must have convinced her that I was clean, and she let me proceed to the next room. Twenty other people waited in detention. The plane was not quite ready.

"Yeah, mon" an attendant said. "The plane not fixed yet. No worry, we fix the plane."

From the window, I could see that the whole motor was out. The cowling was off around the engine. All the skins were removed, and the whole engine was exposed. I took the work of five men to reassemble it correctly in four hours. Without a bathroom, it was not a pleasant wait.

I spent those worrisome hours surrounded by the smell of other fetid passengers, looking out the windows at the incomparable beauty of the island and praying for deliverance. My mind was crazed; I had built an asylum for myself in the corner waiting.

Then there was another call to embark the plane. I was detoured for yet another inspection. "I've already done that," I protested but still I was detained. This time, in another room, with another female security guard.

"Assume the position," she repeated to me.

Mad as an ape, I did as she requested, but first. I threw all my belongings to the ground and kicked open the suitcase. Furiously, I flung my clothes and affects up and down so she could see that I was not hiding any contraband within them.

When I was through with my abusive display, she calmly felt the outer limits of my manhood and declared me suitable for transport.

Once on board, I chose a seat next to the aisle so I would have unobstructed access to the bathroom, which I used immediately. When I returned, there was an announcement to delay the plane for one more passenger. The plane was stuffed to capacity except for the seat next to mine.

The last passenger was a little Jamaican girl, around nineteen, in a frilly white dress. She was a cute little thing—thin, with big breast. She wore no bra and, as I was to learn, had eliminated panties in her traveling ensemble as well. But her long armpit hair had been braided elaborately, showing she had put thought into her appearance after all.

Even at a distance, I could see the sweat come off her in constant streams. She clumsily made her way across me. Her body sliding across mine, lubricated by the runoff of fearful perspiration. Her awkward motions caused here dress to flutter off her body, and I was apprised of the complete formation of her breast and buttocks. These normally private possessions were mine to inspect inches from my face as they flipped out or bounced upward in her resistant attempts to stay seated.

At first, I thought the mad pouring of sweat indicated sickness, but she confided in me that this was her maiden flight. It mollified me briefly that she was not showing signs of an emerging fever, that it was just incommunicable fear. But the effects of fear in the form of unrelenting sweat were just as bad, no matter how transparent the comely form of my seatmate rapidly became. Trapped for hours in the airline terminal with other such malodors passengers, I thought becoming airborne would final relieve me of the proximity to rank fumes. It appeared, uncomfortably engulfed in rising stench, seemed to be one of the hallmarks of my exodus.

Moreover, I was not unaware of my own stink. And because I had spoiled my clothes when I had stomped on them in a vain display in the last inspection room, I had nothing clean to change into. My upset nerves from my interminable wait and the indecent examinations wafter a distinct odor, resolute and sharp, and were equally a foul match to hers. I had no money to buy drinks, so I might intoxicate myself into listlessness, which also contributed to my continued mounting anxiety.

The plane, against all odds and with the betterment of all those lengthy adjustments, finally arose to the sky. In my heart, I was gratefully, praising the Divine Being. But the swift ascension of the plane was not greeted with equal joy from the little lassie. She immediately jumped out of her seat, having unfastened her seat belt against the admonishment of the "Fasten Seat Belt" sign. In her alarm, her adjustments was not recommended by the strict aeronautic board. She took refuge in my arms and in my lap, vulnerable as a lost lamb.

But she did not, I think, look like a lost lamb to the other passengers. She was screaming the extent of her fear, lost in helpless fright. When she was not expressing herself verbally, she was rubbing herself frantically across me, nudging my mouth open with hers. She applied her frantic hands to all parts of my body, in terrified appeal. She hung on to me, clung to me, made the maximum use of my sodden body to sooth hers.

I appealed piteously to the stewardesses, who were not swift in coming. When the plane leveled off so they could safely traverse the aisle, they pried the young woman from me and fed her a calming pill. There, the girl sat, less physically frantic, except for the waterworks, which persisted drenching her completely.

During the flight, I withstood the sniggers of the other passengers as they passed our cozy section. Some were outright in their lewd suggestions.

"Brought you back a little something from Jamaica," they chortled in sophisticated assumption.

I was embarrassed, but I could not abandon my post.

The flight rambled through miles of turbulence, which kept the girl firmly pinned to my side. Together, we withstood the jostling of the tumult in the skies and the sly glances of our fellow travelers. She held my arm while I assumed a brave poise, and together, we breathe in each other's rancid emissions.

When the plane safely landed, I gave my seatmate the quickest of goodbyes, after reassuring her that now that we hand touched terra firma, my assistance would no longer be needed. That said, I sprinted to the head of the pack, one of the first alighting passengers.

At customs, I saw what would soon befall me. The Jamaican traveler in front of me was in the throes of having his suitcase and belongings torn asunder, in yet another lengthy and perhaps fruitless search for dope. We looked at each other, in what I thought was with mutual sympathy. But his eyes were following a distant image, a figure closing in behind me. It was the Jamaican girl running to catch me, breast and buttocks bobbling. Desperate as she was for reunification, I could no longer be her savior, having reached the end of my frayed rope. When she came upon me, embracing me in a most passionate manner, I simply and hard heartedly relinquished all knowledge of her.

"She's not with me," I cried to the customs agent, my fellow passengers, and to the heavens above. "I don't even know her. She was just on the plane."

Then after a few moments of practiced wrestling, I pried her skinny arms off me and dumped my bags violently to the floor.

"I have had it," I declared vehemently. "I am never going to leave the United States again." I pointed to my scattered parcels. "If you wanna take my bags, take the goddamn bags and keep 'em. I don't give a shit no more. I want out of here."

The custom agent took great interest in this emotional dissociation with the girl and my luggage as did the other passengers who seemed greatly entertained by my prolonged saga.

Then the agent said understandingly, "Had a rough flight?" Had a rough time? Bad experience?"

"All the above," I confessed.

With the upmost commiseration, he let me thorough.

"I understand. Go right ahead."

When the driver took me home, I noticed how brown my lawn looked. Apparently, the sprinklers had broken while I was gone, and the grass had died. After the verdant plants of Jamaica, it was quite a change.

My wife, Patti—seeing me wrinkled, sweaty, smelly, and besmirched with lipstick and suspicious bruise marks about my neck and face—could not help but comment. "What the hell have you been doing?" she asked, fending off my kisses. "Either you been doing it, or you had a helluva time."

"Patti," I said at last relieved. "It would take a month to tell you this story, but honest to God, I've been good. I've been good."

Then I took a shower. I scrubbed my body and doused my hide liberally with alcohol. The tropical languor was finally gone.

In the end, the experience was worth the trouble. In show business, the tribulation is always the storyteller's reward. Because like the Dragnet stunt, I did not receive screen credit for my Jamaican ordeal. This account is what I have left of a month shanghaied.

And that was my experience and adventure in the filming of the movie *The Mighty Quinn*, starring Denzel Washington.

Rene in Jamaica

CHAPTER 3

My Greatest Stunt

Dragnet (1987)

Starring Tom Hanks and Dan Aykroyd
Behind the Scenes

THE SIMPLEST STUNT I was ever to do turned out to be the most dangerous stunt I ever did. Life or death!

My brothers called me to do a "little simple job." Just drive our Army tank down the street on a movie called *Dragnet* (1987), starring Dan Aykroyd and Tom Hanks. They told me no big deal.

So I got the big tank out and serviced it completely. You never know what else could happen. I was just supposed to drive the tank through about a foot of fire.

The day came. I loaded the big tank on the transporter, and we were off to the set. When we got to the set, I thought something did not look right. A propane truck was there with a lot of copper propane lines running to a giant twenty-food-wide by at least thirty-foot-wide object.

"What the hell is this?" I asked the stunt coordinator.

He said, "It is going to be a large burning Christmas tree. A lot of fire. Can you make it safe for you, and can you and the tank withstand the fire?"

I said, "Yes, and I need to get a lot of extra protective equipment."

"Go and do it. Get whatever you need."

I drove the police tank in *Dragnet* for Dan Aykroyd and Tom Hanks.

This was actually an Army reconnaissance tank, which was painted the color of the LA police uniform, a dark blue. Most evident was an impressively long battering ram protruding like an elongated penile projectile. Attached to the shaft of the ram was a metal placard with a police shield emblazoned and the proclamation "Have a nice day." The tank had been in storage for a while and needed to be thoroughly checked out and properly sealed, which I attended to myself.

My first scene took place at a milk packaging plant, which was believed to be an illicit warehouse for manufacturing lethal chemicals. This movie had all the familiar cop action elements: two mismatched partners, a gruff supervisor, strippers, car chases, a corrupt politician, a duplicitous clergyman, fights at a bacchanalian orgy, and to prove the principles were heterosexual crime fighters, a virgin sacrifice. But the stunt I was to do was unique. I do not think the storming of a milk processing factory by a tank with a fully extended battering ram had been filmed before.

I listened for my command on my headsets. When the director yelled action, I put my tank into gear. I had three inches in either side to get through the building. The M114 tank could go a frisky forty-five miles an hour, but it had been decided that I was to go at a leisurely fifteen miles an hour so the camera could take its time recording my progress. I bore through the double doors, splintering them. Inside the storeroom, milk sprayed in all directions from the overhanging pipes I had ruptured on my rampage. People caught in the shower of reconstituted dry milk ran helter-skelter, coated with the pearly spray. The plan was that I was to operate the tank uninterruptedly until I encountered the immense vats, which would prove too bulky for me to penetrate completely. My trajectory was to be a straight shot, which, even for a precision tank driver, could be tricky.

However, we did not factor in the effects of the painted floor. The tank was sure-footed on loose rubble, but on a painted floor, apparently it would slide. As I made my way toward the milk vat, the tank began to slip out of control. I realized that my speed was increasing and I was jeopardizing the shot. The tank skidded helplessly like a rhinoceros on ice. I could have damaged the tank if I inadvertently plowed into the side of building as rudimentary physics intends. I knew they needed the tank afterward for a close-up shot of Aykroyd and Hanks emerging from the porthole, and it would not do to show the tank's armor ravaged as the consequence of its assignment. Instead, I made adjustments as quickly as I could, correcting the steering in the opposite direction, shimmying back and forth until I could slow the tank down, creating drag. Evidently, my shrewd swerving worked.

On film, my maneuvers looked erratic yet choreographed for excitement. The tank punctures the dairy like a demented beast unleashed. It appeared that the milk vats were not so much the operators' objective as they were their eventual ruin. This tumult pleased the production staff. I was just trying to prove my mettle as an adept driver by averting disaster.

The next stunt was to perforate the gates of a millionaire pornographer's lair. The location team, in their ironic humor, chose the Catholic monastery on the heights above Los Feliz Boulevard to stand in for the site. When I was first briefed on this shot, I was told the tank would have an obstacle one foot high to scale. This little mound would represent the accumulation of the smutty books and magazines the inhabitants of the manse chose to hurl in their defense. As only bedlam would do, the reading material would be lit like a funeral pyre. I would have to traverse this pile of inflammable material, for as we all know, in the movies, heroics knows no impediments.

Now I knew that a one-foot high campfire would do for a scene with peaceful dancing Marquesan islanders, but for the final showdown between the good guys and the bad guys, only greater pyrotechnics would do. This was also where the secret tank driver, Dan Aykroyd's character, disgraced and disbadged, redeemed himself. The fire would have to be very high to signify his immense dedication to duty in spite of the department's repudiation of him. So I was just waiting for the ante to be upped. When they asked if I could plow through a three-foot fire, I was not surprised. As a rule, those movie guys fiddle quite a bit with perimeters as the filming progresses. Special effects seem to be particularly prone to expanded inspiration. Subtlety is relinquished whenever eruptive bombast will do.

But I admit, I was startled when I arrived on the set and saw a five-thousand-gallon propane truck parked at the bottom of the hill. From a modest fire in a little propane pot, the fire reconfigured tenfold. Somewhere along the line, huge racks had been assembled to create a mammoth Christmas tree–like framework to ignite. The blaze was designed to reach the heights of a thirty-foot conflagration. The extravagant amount of propane supplied was to ensure the combustible heap burned bright and sure.

I was asked once again if I wanted to sign on to this revision. Dazzled but confident, I still agreed. After I regained my composure, I started to make a few minor modifications on my own. Once renegotiated, I asked for additional safety measures. I needed heat-retardant protection, a Nomex suit the same as race car drivers wear, Nomex gloves, and a special nonflammable helmet. I requested an upgraded headset to hear and communicate more effectively instead of the handheld walkie-talkie I had been issued. It was especially important for me to be abreast of direction. With my limited scope inside the vehicle, I would not be able to tell if there was something wrong outside. I had my faith in others to tell me if I had to reroute my course, left, right, or backward.

The fireman assigned to this stunt was asked his insights as well. His first concern was my right mind. Once convinced I was logical and prudent and could surmount the danger, he alerted me to the added hazard of riding in a gasoline-powered machine. The additional fuel could prove to be my further undoing. He ordered it to be drained, except for the amount that would see me on my way. Then the fuel tank was sealed to keep it from mixing with the propane, fire being indiscriminate in its choice of nourishment.

With these details settled, I found my seat in the tank. I was properly outfitted in my antifire ensemble, with my headset and mouthpiece arranged on my head.

I was asked if I was ready. I answered affirmatively, stepping on the gas, clearing out my carburetor. I knew there was no stopping the proceedings once I began my march on the manor. It would be a one-take deal, and no mistakes were permitted. The fire department and water trucks were there to give me aid, but I was on my own to roast in my voluntary crucible.

The fire was lit. Through my peephole, it was all I could see. It was brighter and hotter than a recently crashed meteorite. I aimed the end of my twenty-foot barrel at its molten center. At the call of action, I drove up the hill. I shook in terror, feeling so isolated in my metal encasing like an astronaut jettisoned into unexplored space. Each inch, each accomplishment, I coaxed myself through. I fought against my greater reasoning, diverted myself against the flood of turmoil that was causing my heart to race so. But I could not stop myself from fulfilling my suicide objective.

The hill was scaled. The gates were next. I broke through their wrought iron filigree and left behind a shamble of twisted metal bars. The sound made my stomach drop. There was a slight reprieve between the gate and my last hurdle. The open ground was no relief. It served only to emphasize the significance of my coming folly. Inside my Nomex suit, I began to foam with hot sweat. The flames beckoned me with curling fingers. My foot kept constant contact with the gas.

My momentum could not be stopped. I was drawn to plunge determinedly and unconsciously into the waiting inferno that rose upward toward the evening sky.

I entered the fire's embrace. But the fire's clutches would not release me. I punched the gas, but I was not propelled forward. The tank would not take me forth but was led end on, climbing up an inexplicably obstinate mound. Evidently, the pyramid of fire rested on a pile of boxes filled with plaster. Plaster was used because the fire would extinguish the boxes immediately, and a form was needed to suggest the burning magazines. The plaster boxes, however, could not withstand the massive density of the tank, and they collapsed as soon as its foundation was needed. The tracks ate the plaster, and the tank crawled up. This left my tank and I atop this uncertain fulcrum, hung up, teetering this way and that, in the waving flames.

There was no evidence of the tank outside of the fire. I was engulfed completely. Propane assisted the blaze to form the densest walls, the most absolute corral. I could not even see the gun barrel through the sparks and smoke. The twenty-by-twenty-by-thirty-foot metal and gas conflagration heated to an unbearable temperature. The skin that stuck to my suit began to broil. My mind entertained the outmost extremes of panic. I saw my entire life compacted within a second. I saw my beginning, myself as a baby. I swiftly recounted one span to the next. I felt the excruciating pain of leaving my wife and family. I had the sense of my own death in the hot glow. I wondered where my spirit would be transferred once my body charred.

But then I refused this devouring death. We all thought the boxes would be easy to drive right through. No one expected the tank to ascend the plaster and to lift me up where I was helpless. We judged the fire would be a permeable barrier, not a permanent one. I made up my mind to fight the elements. I came up with a way out.

I turned the tank from side to side, maneuvered the tank right to left. The wheels graded the plaster, chewed it up, grabbing fraction. I smashed the four-foot-high mound of plaster at my loft height and forced myself down. I graded the plaster until it crumbled beneath me. When I came down from the pinnacle, my headset fell to the ground. Voices trying to instruct came through the dense fog of smoke and heat. But I could not return my response. I stopped the tank at the fire's base. I could smell the odor of burnt paint and the rancid stink of the rubber tracks aflame. I had emerged from the fiery fount, but I was still enwrapped in its far-reaching tentacles.

I was ordered to drive straight, fast and quick. I was told I was still on fire and to stay in the tank. I could see the tongues of flame leap sporadically in front of me, coming alive and then diminishing out of no known source. I drove thirty feet past the fire, and still it accompanied me. The stunt coordinator commanded me to stay inside my tank even while it was halted and to move left, right, stop, left. The fire trucks came and doused me with water. I could hear the surge from the hose beating against the metal sides.

But inside it was still blistering. I felt horribly ill. Breathable air was lessening. My lungs uncontrollably swallowed scorching smoke. My head felt dizzy, and I could barely reply to those in control who asked repeatedly if I was all right. The paint, the fumes, the heat, the smoke, the oxygen-poor air all made me begin to lose consciousness. In thirty seconds, I would have tumbled into nothingness. I made myself remain alert because I knew that around me there were two hundred to three hundred people and a sharp cliff. If I became irrational or passed out and accidentally set the acceleration on full bore, I could have damaged much more than just myself and the prop vehicle. And then there was the possibility that the remaining gas in my tank could have exploded even after the surface flames were contained.

When the tank was thoroughly doused in water and foam, the crew began to jump up and down on it, to get the lid open. But they could not because I was locked in, sealed in. Only I could unlock the tank from the inside. When I popped open the lid, the whole assembly was staring down in wonder at me. I was still choking and coughing.

Dan Aykroyd came and swept me into a huge hug. He inquired sincerely if I was okay. And all around me was a chorus of congratulation and admiration. Dan helped me out of the tank and walked off with me, patting me on the back. He offered the use of his dressing room anytime I needed it for the rest of the shoot. In fact, out of his own empathetic feelings, he suggested I go in there and talk to his wife, the beautiful actress, Donna Dixon.

"Just go in and chat with Donna," he urged as if that was what he would do after a near-death experience.

"Thank you, Dan," I said. "Thank you. I'm just fine. I'm just gonna go sit down over there and get some air."

So I sat down, had some water, breathed in air, relaxed, and calmed down. There were forty people around me. The doctor and nurse assigned to the movie checked me over. I was fine. The transportation director told me I did a great job. The director came over and thanked me profusely. He told me it looked real good. He suggested I relax a minute and asked if I needed any water or anything. He brought me some more water.

In another hour, I was up and doing another stunt. There were more technical stunts with the tank, maneuvering, hitting the mark.

I left the impression that I was very daring. They were able to capture the shot perfectly. It was more spectacular than what they had planned, much more than they had bargained for. It was suspenseful to have the tank lost in the fire and eventually come out burning. I had almost lost my life doing it, but I was able to save my own hide as well.

Two years later, I came across Dan Aykroyd on a television talk show. The host was reviewing Dan's experiences in action movies. He was especially impressed with Dan's work in *Dragnet*. The host described in detail the tank demolishing the factory and the scene of Dan's coming to the rescue through the fire courageously. The host found those stunts to be especially exciting.

Dan agreed with him and said, "Yeah, a friend of mine made me look good."

It is always like that for me. Just one shot, one take, do or die, life or death. And it always seems that I get the other end of life or death. That is the way it works for me.

Rene, the tank driver

Rene and Dan Aykroyd

Tank entering milk factory

Tank crashing milk factory

Tank crashing milk factory

Tank going to the fire

Tank in the fire

Tank coming out of the fire

CHAPTER 4

My Most Dangerous Stunts

Behind the Scenes

I GOT A call from my brothers that they were going to do a film shoot for a television show in Japan. The premise of the program was to pit two tanks against each other and race them across an obstacle course. The contestants of the game were supposed to figure out which tank would eventually win. It was like a horse race, but instead of horses, two Army tanks were racing in the contest and doing so over a dangerous and hazardous track. My brothers would provide the vehicles and drive the tanks. And I would be part of the comic relief.

My nephew had the contract to set up the obstacle course and was charged to make it as difficult and challenging as possible. This presented all sorts of merciless possibilities, because short of a snorting toxic monster, nothing would deter an Army tank. The producers wanted the tanks to go over the sharpest turns, the deepest gullies, the highest hills. Anything and everything was greenlighted, as long as it presented the maximum maneuvering difficulty. The ranch in its most natural state provides both undemanding and unyielding terrain, fields, ditches, trees, and waterways. And with a few man-made barriers like cars and signs, all the elements were in place for havoc on the run.

I would have the small but significant role of a construction worker prematurely disrupted from an outhouse visitation. I wore Levi's, a plaid shirt rolled up halfway, work boots, and a hard hat, with a nail belt and hammer slung at my waist. This was not unlike a getup I would have worn on many a day erecting sets on the property. The portable toilet was a typical construction site Andy Gump model, on the low end of the scale, without the faucets for running water or holders for decorative flower vases.

The setup was pure Three Stooges. The script had me meandering into the privy, unaware of the scudding tanks. I would be left to attend to my private matters, ignorant of the danger that was advancing my way. Upon hearing their rumbling motors, I was to evacuate the latrine, but only at the last possible moment. My vulnerability and panic would lend the scene a human perspective. It goes without saying, getting ambushed in a toilet goes right to the heart of all our fears.

The outhouse itself was four feet by four feet by four feet and six and a half feet to seven feet tall. It was light plastic, painted blue, with a little vent at the top. To increase the obstinacy of the

Andy Gump, we nailed the structure to the ground with big stakes. If we had not secured it to the ground, the tanks would have just pushed the building along instead of running over it and smashing it to unrecognizable fragments. Scooting along an outhouse would look cute, but having it chewed up with bits flying around in the procedure would crank up the excitement factor intensely. People in film were always dreaming up how to better dismember parts.

Although, in this incident, I was supposed to be oblivious of my impending doom, I took the precaution of cutting a two-inch-by-two-inch lookout in the back of the toilet. I needed it so I could get a visual clue on the tanks as well as an aural one. The cameras were placed fifty feet in front of me to the side and would not be able to record my little porthole.

I reckoned this would not be a physically difficult stunt. It was all a matter of timing. Too soon, the anticipation would not have a chance to crescendo, and the uproarious finale would be less than galvanizing. To late a flight from the latrine, causing an unplanned collision, and I would have compressed myself ad infinitum in a plastic tomb.

I was situated in the inner sanctum of the Andy Gump when I heard the tanks come rumbling my way. From the sound of them, I could tell they were fifty feet in the distance. They had just rounded a curve and were now on a straightaway. From my experienced ear, I could tell by the reverberation of their engines that they were traveling at twenty-five miles per hour and picking up acceleration. I had not expected this kind of haste. The rate of velocity did not give me much time to make my breakaway. I theorized that my brothers were going so fast because of increased adrenaline and their competitive natures urged them to exceed the determined speed. But I also had darker thoughts as well.

The thunder and clatter of the tanks generated sympathetic creaks and chatters in my private cell. The walls and floor joggled and jounced violently despite the sturdy spikes laid in the foundation. It was like an earthquake had convulsed the surrounding ground, moving me from side to side, shuddering the tiny compartment like a baby rattle.

I positioned my hand on the door handle and jiggled it lightly to test its mechanics. Previously, it opened and closed freely. This time, it would not budge. The plastic door had buckled, trapping the latch. I lifted it again and again. It would not unhinge. The dirt below me vibrated with increasing magnitude. I looked through the hacksaw-cut window. All was a blur of dust and debris. I could hear the tanks, their boom and drone, but I could not see any outline of them. The dirt was thrown up before the cavalcade, obscuring their proximity to me. I could not judge if my brothers were five feet back or ten feet.

There would be no one to intervene in my behalf. The cameramen could not very well run in front of the tanks, flagging their attention to slow down or divert their direction. Even if I did not appear, I had this grisly feeling that my brothers would complete their last dash without interruption, whether or not I had run clear of the target. I wrestled with the door; it was obstinately warped. I did not want to die.

I pushed the door with my shoulder. In concert with the tanks rolling, it pushed back at me. I tried the latch at the same time. It stuck defiantly. I peered through the small back window. It was getting darker as the tanks came closer. I pushed with every ounce of my body. The door remained fastened. My sense of survival had me thinking fast. I stepped back from the entrance of the latrine and leaned against the back wall, using it for leverage. I aimed for the center of the door with my right foot. I had never realized how much power could be contained in one thrust. I put everything I had into that fearful kick. The brute force of my survival instinct forced the door to open finally.

Once outside, the momentum carried me into a dive. The initial plan was for me to stop, look at the tanks barreling toward me, and then give an exaggerated reaction of horror, but I instinctively knew that I had seconds to save my skin. There was no time for a burlesque interlude. As soon as I hit the ground, I lunged as far away from the outhouse as possible and fell into a tuck and roll. I kept in the curled position and rolled and rolled until I was out of the shot. From riding horses and doing fight scenes, I knew how to fall, how to jump, how to protect myself. The weight of a body falling incorrectly could break legs and snap ankles. I performed the tuck and roll automatically, and I did it naturally as I had done a hundred times before.

I was grabbed by a crew member. He pulled me about ten feet more to make sure I remained unharmed. "Man, you cut it pretty close, didn't you?" he said, helping me to my feet.

"Yeah," I answered, "I cut it a little close." I did not tell anyone that the door stuck. It was my stunt. I was responsible for all the prerequisites. I could not have foreseen the door jamming like it did.

Seconds later, the demolition occurred. I watched the two tanks plow through the outhouse, sending it ass over teakettle. My brothers hit hard, forcing the Andy Gump to flip up in the air, plunge to the ground, and wheel helplessly, until they came upon it and ruthlessly flattened it into a crumbled mess. It was plain that it would have been impossible to halt the tanks in their all-out run.

I was dusted off and placed before a camera to record my reaction shot. There were no words in my act, simply a startled expression of terror. My mind recollected the incident once again. It was not the cloud of dirt obscuring my vision, it was not the tremendous pulsation jouncing the outhouse, and it was not the useless latch and the contorted door. It was another memory that made me grimace.

I still remember this stunt today! A friend of mine said he saw me jump out of an Andy Gump plastic toilet, and seconds later, two Army tanks ran over the toilet and destroyed it.

"Boy, you sure cut that one close!"

"Yes," I said, "too close."

In hindsight to this unbelievable true story, I should have turned that job down. With my two brothers driving the Army tanks, it would have been devastating for them to run over their oldest brother, me. I should have known better as I did not have control over the stunt. In all my other stunts, I was the one who had control of myself. The tank drivers could not see me and did not know the door got stuck. They would have run over me and not even know it.

I still have nightmares over that stunt. I am so happy to have made it through that stunt. That's why they call me Lucky Pierre Rene.

Camp Runamuck

Starring Howard Duff
Behind the Scenes

I received a call from my agent to stunt double Howard Duff. The stunt involved fifty Texas longhorn steers in a large pin. He was supposed to run from one side of the pen to another without getting stabbed by one of the steer's horns.

I had never done this before, but I told the production company, "I can do this." Well, after makeup, wardrobe, and stunt pads everywhere, I thought I could be stabbed and covered up by the wardrobe. I was ready after being made up to look like Howard Duff. One more obstacle I had to pass—being approved by Howard Duff. As he came walking over to meet me, I saw a smile on his face. He said, "Perfect. You look just like me. Make me look good in the steer pen, but don't get hurt. I took the precaution to have a medic and ambulance standing by."

I said, "Thank you."

He said one more thing as he took a St. Christopher medal from his neck and put it on me. Then he said, "Here is extra precaution."

I thought that he was a wonderful, thoughtful man. Then the fear set in on me as I thought before every stunt.

Now it was on me to do a good job. As action was called, I was told, "Go for it, Rene."

I jumped over the fence and landed in the pen. The steers look at me and me at them. They began to charge me, and I said to myself, "Oh, shit! What did I get myself into now?" As I dodged the incoming charging steers, I knew if I fell down, it would be all over for me. So I charged back in, out, and around, finally seeing the other side of the pen, and made a run for it as one steer knocked me into the fence as I was climbing over to safety. Made it!

The director called, "Cut! Good job, Rene. Thanks."

Howard Duff came over and said, "Thank you for a great job."

And as I handed him back his St. Christopher medal, I told him, "I could not have done this without your help." So as a stuntman, I defied the law of death again.

Well, that is what we do. That's show business.

CHAPTER 5

When Things Go Wrong

Steele Justice (1987)

Starring Martin Kove and Sela Ward
Behind the Scenes

DID YOU EVER have a bad feeling about something? Well, on this one movie, I did. But being a stuntman in this business, it is pretty much every day you go to work. So you work to overcome this.

In the movie *Steele Justice*, I was to drive a Ferret armored scout car. This was a small Army tank that my two brothers owned. I also was a double for the actor Martin Kove.

I loaded the Ferret tank up on the car carrier transporter and left for location to Long Beach, California. When I got there, I unloaded the Ferret tank and went back for another load of five police cars. I got back to the location and unloaded the police cars and got ready to film.

In the meantime, the armor gun guy asked me to help him load the blanks for the machine gun that went on the tank. Okay, a couple hours went by, and by this time, we had loaded several thousand blank bullets for the actor Martin Kove.

The producer and director came by to check out the tank and machine gun tank.

"Okay, how is the machine gun?"

Martin Kove said, "Let me get the feel of the machine gun. Okay, it is great. Can I fire it?"

The gun guy told him, "It is okay to fire it." He shot and shot; bullet blanks were flying everywhere. He was really enjoying this. Seconds later, he was out of bullets.

The director said, "Let me fire that machine gun." He loaded up and was firing everywhere. Seconds later, he was out of bullets.

Now the producer said he wanted to fire the gun too. He did, and everyone enjoyed firing the machine gun. The gun guy then said he was out of bullets and had to go buy some more. "And oh, by the way, you just shot up five thousand dollars in bullets." The producer and director asked why they were not told to not shoot so much. The gun guy said, "You are the boss, and it is not my job to tell you you can't shoot." I was scared as they started to argue. Bad deal.

"Okay, let's shoot. Rene, warm up the Ferret tank."

Okay, I was inside the tank, and Martin Kove was sitting on top of the tank with his feet on my shoulders.

"Action!"

Martin Kove pressed on my left shoulder to clue me that the tank was to turn left. When he pressed on my right shoulder, I was to turn right.

He was pretending to fire the machine gun, and because he had no bullets, they would dub in the sound of the machine gun after. Everything was going good, maybe too good. Sure enough, on the second take, the damn tank wouldn't start. The shit hit the fan, just like the five thousand dollars in bullets. I jumped out and instructed them to get me a truck and rope. They did, and I tied the rope to the tank and the truck.

"Action!"

The rope broke. *Oh shit, I am in trouble.* "Get me a bigger truck and a steel cable."

They yelled out, "Will that work?"

I said to myself, "I don't know." Then to them, I said, "Yes, yes, it will work, and you can get your shot." I was somewhat of a hero after that. I don't know with old tanks, but no matter how much you work on them and you think you did everything, something always breaks down. Oh well, I left the tank for my two brothers to come and get it.

They used the police cars and were done with them, so I took and loaded them up on the car carrier. By the time I had the police cars loaded, it was about 3:00 a.m. As I left Long Beach in the fog, wet, damp, partly raining conditions, I knew it was a dangerous job to be driving a car carrier with five police cars on it. I had just worked sixteen hours with little rest, but that is what we do.

So as I was driving down the freeway, people were waving at me. Well, I waved back. Then they were yelling out the window, "Your police car is on fire!"

"What? Fire! Oh shit!" I pulled over and got out. Sure enough, one of the police cars had caught fire. I did not know how this happened, but I hurriedly put out the fire with my fire extinguisher I carried on the truck. Boy, was I lucky I got it out before it caught all five police cars on fire. My brothers would not be happy. I did not want to buy five burnt police cars.

Finally, I got back to Newhall at the base transportation lot and went home to crash and wanted to sleep for three days. No luck. I got a call from the brothers to get right over to the transportation lot.

"What is wrong?"

"Get over here, and I will tell you."

I dragged myself over there and asked what was wrong.

They told me, "Number 1, you broke our tank."

I yelled back, "It stopped running!"

"Number 2, who burned our police car up?"

I yelled back, "That was the studio!" (I lied.)

"Number 3, who put all the bullet holes in our police car?"

I said, "What?" Oh my god, as I was driving through Pacoima, I thought I heard a car backfiring. Oh my god, the gangs in Pacoima thought I was hauling real police cars, and they shot the police cars up. I yelled back, "Shit, I could have been killed!" I could have been shot, turned the car carrier over, and had five policy cars go skidding down the freeway. The car carrier would have been upside down and probably hit fifty cars, and I would never see my wife and son again. I told them they were lucky I brought back the car carrier and the cars in one piece. Just a little smoke damage and a few little holes.

To me, that is show business. I knew I had a bad feeling about this show. Well, so lucky no one got hurt, like me. Thank you, God!

To Rene —
The "Tank King"
Regards
and No
"Mercy"
Marty
"Sensei"
Kove

Steele Justice
Martin Kove stars as John Steele, a Vietnam War veteran who battles his way through the underworld of the Los Angeles Vietnamese Mafia, in *Steele Justice* from Atlantic Releasing Corporation.

War Games

Newspaper Reporter Got Shot
Behind the Scenes

At my Blue Cloud Movie Ranch, I do a lot of shows for the retired soldiers' war games. They would come to my ranch always organized by great companies. Usually about eight hundred veterans, enlisted soldiers, and want-to-be soldiers, all very serious about the games. Usually they would divide the soldiers into two groups of soldiers and about one hundred Middle Eastern people. They all were gung ho; everything was real. But the guns they would use were paintball guns. When you were shot, paint would splatter on your uniform, and then you were done. In other words, playtime killed.

This one time, the game was advertised all over the world. I prepared my ranch with Hummers, six-by-six Army trucks, cans, barrels, broken-down and burnt cars, crates, and other miscellaneous debris I could find to spread out and up and down my long, sprawling Middle Eastern town. It was super ready, and I, of course, was going to be driving my Hummer with a model from Russia. She was beautiful in her Russian outfit and, of course, carrying a machine gun. I was totally in my Army attire—helmet, goggles, flak vest, and gun.

Just before we were ready to move out and start the war games, we held our meeting with approximately nine hundred soldiers. After, they started to disburse into the Middle Eastern town and started fighting. Just as I was putting the Russian model in the front seat of my Hummer, a newspaper reporter said he would like to go in my Hummer to get pictures and a story. It was okay with me, but I asked him to get an okay from the producers. He did, and I told him to get into the back seat of the Hummer and stay down and keep all windows up because they were trying to ambush the Hummer and steal the Russian model. Then they would be the winner of the war games.

"I have done this many times before," I told the newspaper reporter. "This is very dangerous. Even though it is fake, it is just as dangerous as it is real."

As we approached the Middle Eastern town in the hot Hummer and now were sweating, I started to drive through the town. Smoke bombs hit the Hummer as the terrorists were running alongside it, shooting machine guns (aka paintball guns), shaking the doors, and trying to get in. I dodged them to go through a fireball, hitting debris to get around and down to the end of the street.

The Russian model was very excited as she was firing out the window. I intentionally was driving very slow to give her the best experience she ever had. The newspaper reporter was excited and was shooting pictures like crazy, especially when a terrorist hung on the Hummer. I dragged him about fifty feet before he fell off. He was so excited he stood up and started to open the turret hatch. I said in a loud voice, "Do not do that! Sit down!" He did not adhere to what I was saying, and I knew if he opened the hatch to the turret, he would surely get shot.

Sure enough, he did. As he pushed his upper body up through the turret and exposed his upper body, he yelled out, "I have been shot!" And he fell back into the Hummer.

I looked at him. He was shot in the neck, and blood was all over his chest and white dress shirt. I was pissed. I yelled at him, "I told you not to do that!" In a panicked voice, he said he was sorry as his wound was getting worse. I immediately radioed, "Mayday, mayday." Asked what was wrong, I replied, "The newspaper reporter got shot, and I am on my way back to base. Have a medic ready."

As I pulled into the base camp, the medic took him out of the Hummer and started working on him. We discovered he was hit in the neck with a red paintball that looked like blood. The medic patched him up with a Band-Aid and told him to go home and write his story. "Wash your white shirt as the red paint will come off." Then the Russian model and I resumed the rest of the game.

This could only happen in the movies. That is why they call it show business.

Rene and his Hummer

Russian model and Rene

Middle Eastern street

Planet of the Apes

Behind the Scenes

In 1968, I got a call from my agent to be a horseman and ride a black stallion in a picture called *Planet of the Apes*, starring Charlton Heston. Little did I know how involved it would be. I arrived at Fox Studios at 3:00 a.m., went into a tent, then endured three hours of makeup, then to the wardrobe for one hour, and came out looking like an ape for fifteen to sixteen hours. Then I traveled to the set (wherever it might be that day). On the first day, around one hundred apes went to Van Nuys Airport, where the studio rented two DC-7B-4 engine airplanes to fly the apes to Page, Arizona, to work in the very hot desert.

As we loaded up, I was a little worried about the condition of the planes. The stewardess assured me they were safe to fly. As I tell you this story, I still can't believe it today. We all got loaded up in two planes. The stewardess advised us to all buckle up as we were ready. The pilot fired up one engine, and it smoked and shook. Then he fired up engine number 2 and number 3. As he was trying to fire up engine number 4, it wouldn't start as we were taxing to the runway. I asked the stewardess about engine number 4 not running. She assured me it would be running before we landed. Not sure I liked that answer.

As we were flying along, I was looking out the window, and then about fifty gallons of oil hit the window. I yelled for the stewardess to tell her about the oil, and she replied, "Oh, that happens all the time. We have plenty more oil in the back of the plane and can refill it up again when we land." Of course, I did not like that!

Three hours later, we landed somewhere in the desert in an abandoned airstrip. As we were pulling up somewhere to get off, I noticed the pilot got the fourth engine running. The plane engines were all shut down, and all the apes made a run for the plane's rear exit, only to tilt the plane's tail and hit the runway. The pilot came running out of the cockpit and said, "Everybody to the front of the plane to level it off. Now one at a time, go down a rope ladder." Again, I did not like that either.

Anyway, all the apes got on buses and traveled way out into the desert where the set and horses were waiting. By the time we got ready to shoot, it was way over one hundred degrees in the ape suit. Now on horses, we made a couple of a couple of practice runs on the horse, then the Animal Humane Society representative told us to get off the horses and put them in the shade while we did another couple of scenes. In between scenes, all of us apes were lying under the trucks for shade.

Thank God the first day was over. Back on the buses to the airstrip in the desert. This time I was put on plane 2. Planes 1 and 2 took off, and we flew back to Van Nuys Airport and landed. But plane 1 was not there. Plane 1 should have landed first. My fear was, all my buddies in that plane had crashed. As I frantically inquired were plane 1 was, the stewardess said, "Oh, he overshot the runway." Oh my god, what a nightmare. Then came the plane, and they landed safely. We were all happy that part was over.

The next day, some others and I were dressed as humans and were being chased by the apes in Malibu, California, in a cornfield. I was running with long black hair, no shirt, loincloth around my waist, and wearing sandals. I was being beat by the cornstalks and dirt.

The next day was a real zinger. About seventy-five apes on horses would chase the humans that was us yesterday. Today, we were doing the chase scenes. So we would line up on our horses at one end of the cornfields, and when the director called action, we would ride as fast as we could, pretending we were chasing the humans. It was bad enough getting on the horses while two wranglers held the horse's head so the horse would not see the apes. Yes, we all got thrown from the horses once or twice.

Finally, the last shot of the day was ready. We were all lined up and ready to go. Adrenaline was running high; horses were jumping around. The director called action, and we took off. Imagine seventy-five black horses with apes on their backs! The horses took off like a bat out of hell, and we were racing through the cornfields as fast as the horses could run. I said to myself, "I will be glad when this is over." Just before the end of the chase scene, my horse's bridle fell off the horse. Holy moly, I had no way to control the horse, and it was totally out of control. We came to the end of the shot, and I was yelling to the other ape horsemen that my horse had lost his bridle.

"Help me! Help me! Sandwich my horse in between yours and try to slow me down." Thankfully, that worked, and the wranglers got to the end of the cornfield to lasso my horse and save me. God only knows if this did not work, what would have happened to me. They said "Great job" to me and printed the shot. They did not even realize there had been a problem.

After that shot and getting back to base camp, I said to myself, "Okay, I made it, and this is my last day. Thank God."

However, that was not the story. The assistant director said, "All you apes line up. I have something to tell you. Number 1, you apes, I mean guys, did a fantastic job, and we at Fox Studios thank you. Number 2, bad news, your wardrobe guy, the guy you know helped you get your ape costume on, came down with hepatitis." We all just stood there with our jaws dropped to the ground. What the hell! "You all need hepatitis shots, known as a double shot of gamma globulin, in the ass, then you can go home."

We were all saying, "You have to be kidding."

"No kidding. The nurses and medical trailer is here. Line up, apes." And we went in one door. The nurse pulled our pants down, and we got a shot in each cheek of our ass. Only one good thing about that was, we still had our ape mask on.

Well, that was an experience on that show. Later on, Fox Studios gave me the ape outfit and mask so that I could do rodeos and appearances for the Santa Clarita Chamber of Commerce. Well, maybe I had the last laugh, doing performances as Charlie the Ape.

Rene Veluzat in *Planet of the Apes*

Rene Veluzat in *Planet of the Apes*

Rene as a human in *Planet of the Apes*

Rene Veluzat in *Planet of the Apes*

Rene entertaining at the Chamber of Commerce

Rene's plane and dirt runway

Knots Landing TV Series

Behind the Scenes

I was working as a Hollywood studio driver, Local 399, on this particular job, and I was driving a car carrier, hauling the stars' and casts' cars to the locations. This was for the TV series *Knots Landing*. We were filming on Ventura Boulevard in Sherman Oaks, California. The scene was for one of the cars I brought on the car carrier. It was for a young housewife with her hair rolled up in curlers to just drive down the street and hit a dummy the prop people had tied down on the street. To set the scene, the police department shut down the street for this big shot. While the people rigged the dummy on the street, by tying it to the asphalt with wires, the assistant director cleared the busy street and stores.

Okay, everything was ready for this big stunt to take place. The street was clear; nobody was coming out of the stores. And the stunt girl was ready. The director yelled action to the stunt girl. The stunt girl must have gotten her adrenaline up as she took off really fast. As all the crew, cameras, and I were on the other side of the street watching, I said to myself, "She is going way to fast."

Suddenly, the whole crew realized this and prepared for something to go wrong. Well, it did go wrong! She hit the dummy so hard and fast the dummy rolled over the bumper, onto the hood, and then to the windshield. This broke the dummy all to hell. The head of the dummy came flying off and skidded down the street and gutter.

And would you just know it, two elderly ladies just then came out of one of the stores as the dummy's head came skidding down the curb and came to rest in front of the two ladies. Well, of course, the ladies thought it was real, and both passed out on the curb.

All was well when the ladies were revived and told it was just a movie prop and the stunt went wrong.

Preparing for a Job—Pancho Villa

I always had a fascination with guns as I grew up on a cattle ranch. We all carried guns. As I got older, my dad, for my birthday, bought me a new rifle to go deer hunting. I remember very well my dad buying a new 1963 pickup truck so we could go hunting. So one day, around dusk, we went hunting and drove into a canyon, looking for deer. As we were walking along, my dad spotted one, and he said to me, "Son, get the deer in the sight of your gun and pull the trigger." The deer started walking, and my dad said, "Shoot the deer and keep walking." As I was following the deer with my gun, my dad kept shouting, "Shoot! Shoot!" The deer froze and looked at me with those big brown eyes. I knew I could never kill it. My dad kept urging me to shoot. So I shot, but I put a big hole in my dad's new truck. Well, that was that and the last time my dad took me hunting.

Now for a story that is so unreal but true.

It was a beautiful day, a couple of days before Christmas, in 1994. I had nothing to do for a couple of hours, so I decided to go to the ranch and practice with my new gun I had just purchased. Then the plan was to take my wife, Patti, and son, Marcel, to get our tree for Christmas.

As I arrived at the ranch, I decided I would practice my quick draw. I was scheduled to double the actor Larry Storch on a Western show as a Mexican bandit. So I got all dressed up in my Mexican bandit outfit. As I came out of my wardrobe closet, I looked and felt like a real Mexican bandit. I was dressed in my brown Mexican boots with big spurs, my bandolier with bullets around my neck, a big scarf, and a hat. Now for my prize, my best quick draw holster and my new pistol.

As I walked out into the field, my spurs clicking and strutting like a gunfighter, I would throw three beer cans in the dirt in front of me and pull out my new pistol, load it up, and spin the chamber. Now I was ready. I pulled the pistol out of the holster and fired three times, hitting the cans each time. Now I thought to myself, *I am really good and really feeling the part.*

We had a caretaker for the ranch, Floyd, and I did not realize he was watching me put on the show. He came over and said I was looking good in my Pancho Villa outfit with all my bullets and pistol. He asked if he could shoot my pistol and to see if he could hit the cans just like me.

"I don't know," I said. "It is dangerous." But he finally convinced me to let him try. As I pulled my pistol out of the quick draw holster, I put one bullet in the chamber, and then he stepped forward and fired, missing the can by a mile. So I took the pistol back and said, "Here is how you do this."

I loaded up six bullets in the chamber and spun the cylinder as they do in the movies. Then I flipped the gun around my fingers and then into the holster, ready to draw the gun at lighting speed. As I reached for the pistol in the holster at lighting speed, I thought I had pulled the gun, but instead, unfortunately, I pulled the trigger before I got the gun out of my holster. The caretaker jumped back as blood shot through the air and soaked into my pants. There was a big hole and lots of blood spewing out of my pants. I suddenly realized I had shot myself.

The caretaker completely freaked out, saying, "I did not see you pull the gun."

"I know," I said. "I shot myself." I tried to be calm and not panic. I did not know what to do. What would John Wayne do? He would lie on the ground and try to stop the bleeding. I did try to be calm. Floyd then pulled my boot out of my pant leg, which was filling with blood. I took off my bandana and wrapped it around my leg as hard as I could stand. I was still bleeding and knew I needed to get to the hospital quick, or I could bleed out and die.

I yelled to Floyd, the caretaker, to get my truck, load me in, and race to the hospital. He finally got me in the truck, and off we went. I told him to just run through the gate; I would fix it later. I could tell he was petrified, but knowing him for thirty years, I affirmed that he was a good friend for what he done for me.

As we finally drove four miles of dirt road out of the ranch, we finally got on the highway to the hospital. As we were traveling, wouldn't you know, we hit all the red lights. I told Floyd, "Put your hazard lights on and just run the lights." I tried to call the hospital on the way but misdialed and got a real estate office by mistake. All they wanted to do was sell me a house. No help. On the way, we passed a fire engine and a sheriff. They were all going the wrong way.

We finally got to the hospital, and I asked Floyd to drive up to emergency, run in, and say "Gunshot wound" and then go park the truck. The emergency nurses and ER doctors immediately took my now weak body on a stretcher into the ER and started the procedure to stop the bleeding. On a funny note, as the nurse was removing my bloody sock, she asked if I wanted to keep the sock. "Oh, no, thanks," I replied. As she was throwing the sock away, she heard a clink from the sock. It was the bullet that went through my leg and landed in my sock.

Just then, two sheriff deputies came to my bedside as the hospital had reported a gunshot, as required by law. They then asked me who shot me and if it was the man who brought me in who was waiting in the waiting room.

"Oh no, he saved my life and was there when it happened." Thank God Floyd was there. Not sure I could have made it by myself. I was embarrassed to admit I had shot myself. I explained what had happened. They wrote a report and left, telling his partner that I had shot myself and to let the caretaker go.

This is one story of my life that seems unbelievable, but it all happened to me. That is why they call me Lucky Pierre (my middle name is Pierre) after surviving numerous car wrecks, stunts, crashed helicopters, and the most dangerous stunt that took all my skills, which I did while shooting *Dragnet* (1987). I drove the tank through that large fire. Let me say this, if it was not for the caretaker Floyd Caberra, I probably would not be here today. So a big thank you to Floyd.

Now back to my story. It was not over yet. The caretaker went home and called everybody and told them what had happened. Everyone, that is, except my wife, Patti, who was waiting at home for us to go shop for a Christmas tree. My nephew picked me up in my truck, and then the phone started to ring with my wife asking, "Where are you? You are late getting home, and you promised we would get our tree today."

I said, "Sorry. I will meet you at the tree lot close to our home." I told her to pick out the tree she wanted and I would be there soon. They picked out a big one! The young guy at the lot was struggling with the tree to get the bottom cut off evenly.

Patti, not knowing what had happened, was upset with me as I was not helping the poor guy with the tree. She told me to get out of the truck and help him. I told her I couldn't. "Why not?" Now she was irritated. She came over to the truck and looked in at me and asked me what happened. Then the whole story came out. She was stunned. I told her to just get me home as I was in pain. When we got home, they dragged the tree inside and stood it up. It immediately fell over as she was right—the kid at the lot did not know what he was doing.

Now I could go to bed as I was exhausted and in pain. Patti gave me a bell to ring should I need something. My son Marcel (who was about fourteen years old) came in and told me the tree wouldn't stand up. I told him to go into the garage and get my screw gun, screws, and some long skinny boards. He got them for me, and I dragged myself down the hall. We struggled to get the tree upright as I screwed the boards to the tree and, yes, then screwed them right down to the floor. What was I going to do? Not good, but it worked, and the tree got decorated. It was a Christmas I wouldn't soon forget.

The hospital told me to see my own doctor the next day. I did, and as he was examining me, he told me to go immediately back to the hospital as he suspected gangrene was setting in. I freaked out, and eleven days later, I was released from the hospital. All healed well. I was so lucky the bullet did not hit any bone but just passed through my calf. Patti had the bullet made into a necklace for me. Ha ha. Again, I was so lucky that day.

Murphy's Law (1986)

Charles Bronson's Helicopter Crash
Behind the Scenes

In 1986, I got a job with Cannon Films to build a barn that a helicopter could land on. The show was called *Murphy's Law*, starring Charles Bronson. This was great. I used to stunt double Charles Bronson in the old days at Universal Studios. My title on this show was construction coordinator.

Originally, the stunt called for Charles to run out of fuel and land in a lake. Charles decided he did not want to film in the lake water for a week. So they changed the script to have him land on a barn in the woods. It was my job to build this big barn. I got my crew together and built the barn. They loved it! They had two helicopters to use—the real one to fly around and simulate landing on the barn and the fake mock-up to drop through the barn. The scene called for the helicopter to fall straight down in the barn and then for Charles to get out.

Okay, the real helicopter flew around in the scene; all was going great. Now they brought in the mock-up helicopter. A one-hundred-foot crane lifted the mock-up helicopter way up in the air. The director said, "Wait a minute, we can see the helicopter blades. We need them to turn." The special effects guy said he was not told that. The director said, "Well, I am telling you now. Make the blades turn!"

"Okay, okay," the special effects guy went and bought twenty-five car batteries, hooked them up, and the blades turned now.

Okay, everybody was ready to film. They lifted the helicopter one hundred feet in the air. The director said action, and the special effects guy was ready to push the button so the blades would turn. He pushed the button, helicopter blades are turning, everything is going good, and then sparks from the helicopter are shooting out the window. The helicopter caught on fire. We could not believe what we were seeing. They dropped the helicopter down and put out the fire.

The director yelled, "What the hell just happened?" He told the special effects guy to fix the mess and make the blades turn for the shot.

Okay, so on to plan B. He rigged a one-hundred-foot rope around the shaft of the helicopter blades, wound it up like a top, lifted the helicopter up, and pulled on the rope. "That will work. Great, let's do it."

They lifted the helicopter up in the air. The director called for seven cameras to roll and called action. Fifteen guys were running, pulling the rope. Everything was going good but one thing. When they pulled the rope, they also pulled the helicopter off-center as it swayed from side to side. The director told them to drop the helicopter through the barn. "Quick, we are running out of film." The director told them, "Drop it now!" The special effects guy dropped the helicopter but off-center of the barn. The helicopter came crashing through the barn and landed on its side. The director yelled, "Disaster! It is a wrap. Everybody go home."

I was very unhappy to see the stunt go wrong. We all put a lot of work in it. I was called to the set and told that I needed to repair the barn over the weekend. He said he wanted for the barn to be repaired when they came in on Monday morning so they could reshoot the scene on Monday.

Okay, so I doubled my crew of twenty carpenters and finished the repairs over the weekend. I almost killed myself and my crew to get the barn finished on time. They were happy and finished the shoot with no problems. They thanked me with a big, big bonus and big, big screen credit, in large letters, "Construction coordinator, Rene Veluzat." Just one of the many "hats" I wear.

Tremors (1990)

Behind the Scenes

I am one of the luckiest guys in the world to have worked in the motion picture business in all phases of the business. The exciting thing is, you never know if you are going to get a job. Just kidding! I always have a lot of work. I guess it is because I know how to do a lot of things in the business. You never know what show and who you are going to double or where you are going to go in this world and what you are going to do. I always have a lot of excitement no matter what.

Well, this one show called me to double Michael Gross on a movie called *Tremors*. I was to be in a gun turret mounted on the back of a six-by-six military cargo truck coming down a huge mesa hill, firing all four .50-caliber machine guns at the big worm. At the same time, the production company borrowed this big military turret with four .50-caliber machine guns off a Navy PT boat. They mounted the big gun turret on the back of this Army cargo truck. Now we were ready to shoot. I arrived at the film location shoot in Castaic, California, changed into my double clothes, and waited for nightfall to shoot.

As the night approached, we were taken up this huge very flat hill called a mesa. We did a little bit of filming, but the director wanted it to be real dark. So at 3:00 a.m., he told us we were ready to shoot the big scene. They got me into the gun turret and loaded it up with full blank loads of bullets (full loads are the lowest). Just before they called action, I took a deep breath because I was hyped up to do this, even though I had done this in my mind, rehearsing this stunt to get it right. I knew I was ready. I signaled to the director I was ready, and he called action. The driver took off driving the Army truck down the hill as I commenced firing all four .50-caliber machine guns. The truck was bouncing all over the place as I was being shook from side to side. My stunt straps were holding me to the seat. As I was firing, shells were flying out of the machine gun, and the smoke was almost choking me. I felt good about this scene, and I thought the director was going to like it. I really liked firing those machine guns.

We came to the end of our big scene at the bottom of the hill, and the director was yelling, "Cut! Cut! That was perfect. You did a good job. Thank you."

The actor Michael Gross came over to me and told me, "Thank you for making me look good." I told him he was welcome.

Well, we did not expect what happened next. Down below us in the valley, lights came on, sirens were going off, searchlights were searching the sky, and helicopters were circling overhead. We all started to get scared. *What the hell is happening?* The crew and I were taking cover, wondering what was happening. Ten police cars circled us and told us, "Put your hands up, all of you." We all put our hands in the air but wondered what was going on. We were told we were caught trying to break the prisoners out of the Castaic prison down there. We told them we were just there making a movie.

The cops said as more cops and the SWAT team arrived, "Did you know it is 3:00 a.m.? You are causing chaos by waking up the whole town of Castaic. And now the prisoners are rioting, thinking it was a prison break. And you tell us you are just making a movie."

"Yes, yes, we are."

"Who told you to shoot and make all this noise?"

We all replied, "The director." Well, after much explaining by the director, he did not go to jail.

Well, what an experience that was. That is why they call it show business.

Alias TV Series (2001)

Starring Jennifer Garner
Behind the Scenes

Well, another great day to film at my movie ranch Blue Cloud. And a great day to have the *Alias* TV show, starring Jennifer Garner come here. They had rented my Cessna airplane for the scene. The scene was, the Cessna airplane just landed on my dirt runway, which I had graded for the scene. The airplane propeller stopped turning, and two men got out and walked down the dirt runway, talking. That was the scene.

For this scene, my son Marcel (site rep) and I polished and shined up the airplane. The day came, and they had Marcel pull the airplane down to the runway. Just before they shoot, the director said, "The plane looks too new and shiny." Then came the painter, and the director told him, "Age it down heavy and make it look old." So the painter went to work. A half hour later, the plane looked fifty years old.

I told Marcel, "Now we have a plane that looks like the one I flew out of Jamaica in."

He said, "Ya mon." I told him to cut it out.

The director came over and looked the plane over and said, "Perfect, let's shoot."

Now in the movie business, you can have a brand-new Cadillac, and they will say age it down. Go figure.

Okay, they shot the scene all day. Finally, they said, "Rene, come and get your plane."

"Okay, we will get it now."

Marcel said, "Dad, we pulled the plane down by hand. Let's use your new Ford F-150 truck to pull the plane back to the hangar."

"Okay, sounds good, as it is uphill all the way to the hangar."

I backed up my new Ford F-150 down to the plane. Marcel hooked the tow bar to my hitch, got in the truck, and said "Let's go." I asked him if he tied the tow bar on good so it would not slip off. He replied, "Dad, we are going uphill. It is not going to slip off."

"Well, okay." I was pulling the airplane very slow, and as I approached the airplane hangar, just feet from pulling the airplane inside the hangar, we were hit with a gust of wind, like a small tornado. The wind hit the airplane, and it lunged. The nose cone and propeller crashed into my new Ford F-150, making a giant hole in the new truck's tailgate. The jolt was pretty powerful. After all, an airplane just crashed into my truck.

Marcel said, "Oh my god, Dad, do not get out of the truck. I will check."

I got out anyway as over two hundred extras in the show were watching. We quickly disconnected the airplane from the truck and pulled it into the hangar and locked the door. I drove around and parked in the parking lot. I said to Marcel, "What the hell just happened?"

He said, "Well, Dad, no one will believe it, but tell your auto body man an airplane just flew into the back of your truck."

I did, and he did not believe me. So I said I backed into a large rock. He said that was more like it. "You studio guys are always backing into things."

Well, all the airplane rental money went to fix my truck and then some. I did not get to speak to Jennifer Garner but waved to her, and she waved back. So that was okay. Some days are better than others. Marcel said he was sorry and he would tie the airplane down better next time.

The show went very good after that, and they thanked me for a great day. That meant a lot to me. So that is show business behind the scenes.

Airplane that crashed into Rene's new truck

CHAPTER 6

Doogie Howser, MD

Starring Neil Patrick Harris

Behind the Scenes
Short Stories

I GOT A casting call to work on the TV series *Doogie Howser*, starring Neil Patrick Harris, to play a Mexican bus driver in Mexico, where Doogie played a medical doctor who was going to Mexico to help with a medical emergency.

The scene was Doogie Howser was riding on a Mexican bus in Mexico to the town where the medical crisis was happening. It was a very hot day, over one hundred degrees on the set location. But before the filming, I had to prep the bus, see that it ran good, and prep the road where the bus was to come into the Mexican town. I had to take a backhoe tractor and dig out the road under the Mexican arches where the bus was supposed to come into town.

Well, they day came, and I pulled up in this old ratty, beat-up, no air-conditioning, engine-smoking bus. People on the set said, "Oh my god, what a great bus."

Neil Patrick Harris inspected the bus and me in my Mexican bus driver outfit and said. "This is great."

The assistant director told me to go get in the shade to cool off as it was so hot. "Go have a cold drink while we prep the bus with props, people, animals, and luggage."

Okay, a half hour later, I observed the prop people finishing their job. Sixteen Mexican passengers, men and women, were in their seats ready to go, and luggage piled on top of the bus. We were ready, but there was a flag on the play.

"It will be a few more minutes. Rene, go get in the shade."

Okay, twenty minutes later, I asked the assistant director if he was ready yet. He said no. I said, "You should get all those people out of the bus too for a break and water. They have got to be very hot."

He said, "They will be okay."

Another twenty minutes went by, and they were still not ready. Now I was really upset as the people were still on the bus. I told him, "Okay, get those poor people off that bus as they are going to get real sick. It has to be 110 degrees out here." He just laughed at me. That did it! I went to the producer and told him about those poor Mexican people being left in the very hot bus. He freaked out too and stormed off, saying he would take care of it. As he stormed off, I could see him talking and screaming at the assistant director for treating those people that way. Then they all started laughing, and the whole crew started to laugh too!

He came to me and said, "Okay, Rene, we will take the people off the bus." Next, I saw the prop people going into the bus and removing the sixteen cardboard people. The people I was so worried about were not real, just real-looking cardboard cutouts. The joke was on me! I was so embarrassed!

The assistant director said, "Load up all of the people. And, Rene, get on the bus and get ready for filming."

I was on the bus with sixteen cardboard people, then they put the chickens in cages on the roof of the bus and brought in two pigs and four goats into the bus. Now Doogie Howser said, "Wow."

The director said by walkie-talkie, "Rene, back up the bus up the hill, and let me know when you are ready."

I turned to the sixteen cardboard people, two pigs, four goats, and Doogie Howser and said, "Are you ready?"

Doogie laughed and said, "Yes, let's go." I backed up, and we were ready to go.

We heard over the walkie-talkie, "Action, Rene."

I then started to drive the bus down the winding hill and over the bumpy road. "Hang on!" As we approached the arches and under them, we came to a stop. As the camera was rolling, Doogie Howser stepped off and walked out and walked through a crowd of people as they were cheering, "El doctor is here!"

The director said, "Cut! Beautiful, print it."

The assistant director said, "Doogie, go to your cool dressing room."

Neil Patrick Harris came over to me, shook my hand, and said, "Thank you very much."

He left, and I was told, "Thank you, and you are done."

As the prop people and animal wranglers unloaded their props, pigs, and goats, the prop people said to me, "Rene, you have been such a good sport. Go ahead and keep all those cardboard people." I said thanks and drove off in the bus.

The irony is, I still have those sixteen cardboard cutouts. Today, as I display them periodically, I set the one that looks like me in my desk chair at my office. I have heard some people say, "Rene sure works some long hours. He has been at his desk at work all hours of the night." Maybe I am getting the last laugh.

Doogie Howser, MD bus

National Security (2003)

Starring Martin Lawrence
Behind the Scenes

One of the funniest shows I did at my 50's Town location was *National Security*, starring Martin Lawrence and Steve Zahn. They were two security guards always bumbling and screwing up. My job on this movie was to coordinate the movie at my 50's Town location.

First, they wanted to make Martin Lawrence happy. They asked me to put in a one-hundred-foot-by-one-hundred-foot paved basketball court and also, for his million-dollar motor home, his sixty-five-foot semitrailer for his gym, a pad for his private makeup and wardrobe department, and a pad for his private security team to personally guard him. They asked me if there was cell phone reception at our location. I told them no. I was then asked if I could make that happen. "Oh yes, I can," I told them, and I did everything else.

So I ordered a bulldozer and dozer operator to cut a road to the top of the hill to put in a cell site just for Martin Lawrence. All done, what if the cell site does not work? I was told I should also put one on the other mountain. I said to myself, "It is Martin Lawrence's money. No problem." We tried out the two cell towers, and they both worked perfectly. They were very happy with my work.

The next challenge they gave me was to build a church at the end of town—three sides and leave the back open. So the joke was, Martin Lawrence accidentally drove his police car through the back of the church and way out into the street, crashing through the church windows. To do this, I had to build the church first and then put in three hundred feet of flat street so the stuntman doubling Martin could get up a lot of speed to crash through the church. The ramp that propelled him up and through the huge front window had to be perfect. It was, and the stunt went perfect. I was a hero for what I did on the show. There were numerous stunts, and they all went perfectly, even the one I worried about. Martin's police car hit about ten fifty-five-gallon drums filled with gasoline for a huge explosion. All went well.

As the show was filming in town, in front of Martin Lawrence's camp, I had the water truck wet down the road every half hour so there was no dust to disturb him. Every shot he was in, the limo pulled up to his camp where there was a six-foot fence around it with blackout canvas for his privacy. He came out of his million-dollar motor home and walked fifty feet on red carpet to the limo so his personal driver could take him to the set.

About the third day into the shoot, I noticed a flatbed truck come to the ranch with four motorcycle quads for dirt bike riding. I said to the assistant director, "What is happening? What are the dirt bikes for?" I was told that Martin Lawrence liked the ranch, and they wanted to go dirt bike riding up and down the roads and hills for pleasure. Well, this rubbed me the wrong way, and I told the assistant director that no one asked me, the owner of the ranch, if he could go dirt bike riding and tear up the roads and leave trails in the beautiful mountain terrain.

So now we had a problem. I thought things were going too good. Now there was a problem. What could we do to fix the problem? The assistant was frantic as I told him not to take the dirt bikes off the truck. He left, and I just thought, *The shit has hit the fan,* when he talked to Martin Lawrence. A half hour later, I got called to the set. I was worried. *What the hell is going to happen?* I got to the set, and standing in the middle of the street was Martin Lawrence with ten bodyguards. The crew had stopped work and was sitting down.

Martin Lawrence said to me, "I like your movie town, and thanks for taking care of me. I would like to dirt bike ride down your dirt roads. Can I have your permission?"

I said, "Yes, you can."

He smiled and said, "Thank you."

I said, "Oh, Mr. Lawrence, there is one more thing." Everybody froze in their tracks. What the hell now? "Ah, Mr. Lawrence, I would love to have an autographed picture of you."

He looked at me, smiled, and said, "No problem."

Later, his bodyguard brought me this nice picture of him.

The director personally came over and thanked me for a great job of running the 50's Town Movie Ranch. I thanked him and said, "I have a question. How much money is Martin Lawrence worth?"

"Oh my god, millions, why?"

"Well, to protect Martin and your picture, I would advise you to get Martin a crash helmet while he is riding his dirt bike fifty miles an hour on the dirt roads."

"Oh my god, you are right," he replied. "Driver, go out and get Martin Lawrence a crash helmet." He came back with forty crash helmets.

"We only need one," I told the driver.

He replied, "Yes, but what color, what size, and most of all, which one will he like?"

All ended well. I loved that movie. It was so funny, and most of all, it worked well at my 50's Town Movie Ranch.

My Time with Elvis Presley

Behind the Scenes

I got a call to be on a movie with Elvis Presley. Man, was I excited! He was a huge movie star, and I wanted to meet him. I did, and we talked a lot about Tennessee. He seemed to like me, and I let him know my dad was from Tennessee. I worked on about ten of his movies. We became good friends. In fact, he offered for me to be one of his boys and move back to Memphis with him. Man, I so wanted to do that, and I pondered that offer. But I was married at the time, and I had to sadly tell him I could not make it. He said, "Well, let me know down the road if you get divorced and want to go with me." So I thanked him.

Whenever he came to town to make a movie, I was always on the set. It was a good day with Elvis every day I worked with him. He was funny and played a lot of tricks on his friends. When we were doing a fight scene with the actor L. Q. Jones, Elvis broke the actor's leg. Oh, man, Elvis had doctors, nurses, and assistants taking care of L. Q. Jones full-time while he was working. But Elvis still pulled tricks on the poor actor. He was a good sport and didn't make a big deal out of the pranks as Elvis, his boys, and the crew and myself all joined in the laughter.

While L. Q. Jones was in between takes and resting in his dressing room, Elvis would open the door and throw in a noise made to scare him. While L. Q. Jones was on crutches and he left them outside his dressing room door, Elvis would sneak up and adjust the crutches all the way up. When L. Q. Jones was called to the set, he hurriedly put the crutches over his arms and take a step. He would then swing in midair and fall down. Then we all swept in, picked him up, and carried him to the set. Everybody got a good laugh. When the show was over, he rewarded L. Q. Jones with a very expensive gift.

On one of the Elvis shows I was on, during a break from filming, Elvis would play with one of his toys, a new blue-and-white Harley-Davidson. While he was riding around on the set, a whole crew was watching, including me. He pulled up in front of me and my buddy who doubled for Robert Redford. Elvis said to me, "Rene, how would you like to have my Harley?"

I said, "Oh my god, I couldn't take your Harley, Elvis."

He said, "But I want to give it to you."

I replied, "Elvis, I don't think I could ride that big Harley, but I appreciate the offer."

As he rode off, my buddy said, "You are crazy. You should have taken his Harley. He likes you."

Well, in those days, I was timid. In the studio in those days, you did not ask for autographs or pictures. No cameras were allowed on the job. Now it is different; cell phone cameras take all kinds of pictures of the stars. Now did I regret my choice? Well, maybe. The Harley was now in the Elvis

Presley Museum in Memphis, Tennessee. All the times I was with Elvis, I never asked for anything. I regret not having a picture with us together.

Ironically, my wife Patti and I were on vacation in Hawaii and having a great time. In the market, we saw a sign advertising Elvis Presley and Madonna impersonators. We decided to go see the show. As Elvis was doing his show, he asked for a volunteer from the audience to come up on stage. No one volunteered, so he came to the audience and picked me. As we went on stage, he started singing to me, joking with me, and then he gave me his glasses and scarf and took a picture of him and me. I just could not believe this! Here I never asked Elvis for a picture, and then I went to Hawaii and got the picture I always wanted.

Finally, as his show was over, he said, "Boy, where are you from?"

I said, "California."

He said, "Where?"

And I said, "A little town you probably never heard of, Newhall."

He said, "I can't believe this either. I live in Saugus, California, two miles from Newhall."

I told him I worked on many Elvis movies and never asked for anything. I thanked him profusely for letting me finally get my Elvis picture.

As I was leaving, I chuckled to myself. What were the odds? He did not give me a Harley-Davidson, but I was happy with what I got.

MacGyver (1985)

Starring Richard Dean Anderson
Behind the Scenes

One of the great original shows was *MacGyver*, which I had the privilege to work on. Richard Dean Anderson was great to work with. He was friendly with everybody, and he was a jokester. He played tricks on people. Probably one of the biggest, funniest, but serious jokes he played was on the makeup girl.

Richard and I talked every day. On his show, there were always bombs and lots of special effects. On the *MacGyver* series, I was hired to drive a water truck for fire protection. At any minute or any time of the shooting day, I was responsible if any fire broke out on the set or any special effects went wrong. I would be needed to rush in with my water truck and put out the fire. We always were filming outside, always near the brush. Thank goodness nothing ever went wrong requiring my services.

Well, I noticed that Richard and the makeup girl, who was very attractive, would play tricks on each other. This went on every day, something new every day. Then one day, the makeup girl sneaked up behind Richard and put an ice cube down his shirt. He jumped up and shook the cube of ice out of his shirt. He and everyone laughed. Later that day, Richard sneaked up behind the makeup girl and dropped a bunch of ice cubes in her blouse. She jumped up and shook them out. Again, we all had a big laugh.

The next day, the makeup girl poured a cup of water down Richard's shirt. Everyone laughed but the wardrobe guy. He had to get a new shirt for Richard. Oh boy, this was escalating! What next? Later, Richard poured a gallon of water on her and on her blouse. Now this was not funny, and the crew cringed. Later that day, the makeup girl sneaked up behind Richard and poured five gallons of water on him. That was huge! Now Richard was not happy.

The next day, Richard called me over and told me what he wanted me to do. He told me to unwind two hundred feet of fire hose and coil it by his chair. "Okay, Richard," I said, not knowing what he was up to. He gave me a walkie-talkie and told me to stay in the water truck, and when he told me to, he wanted me to start up the truck and give him full water pressure. "Okay, Richard."

A little while later, he called for me to give him full pressure. I said okay and turned it on full blast. I heard a lot of yelling on the set. Then Richard yelled out for me to cut the water, roll up the hose, and come on over. I had no idea what had happened. A crew member told me the makeup girl came walking by, and that was when Richard had said, "Okay, give me water." He chased the poor makeup girl two hundred feet and was spraying her with water all the way. I was told it blew her top off. Later, they came to a truce and made up, agreed to no more pranks or jokes. I was hiding all this time. I felt bad for the makeup girl.

Wouldn't you just know it, ten years later, on a different show, the same makeup girl came over and said to me, "Aren't you that water truck driver on the *MacGyver* show?" I froze in my tracks. She said she was not mad at me, that she knew Richard had put me up to it. I told her I was so sorry. She told me after ten years, she was not mad anymore. I was so relieved, and we both had a good laugh about it.

MACGYVER

HONEST ABE

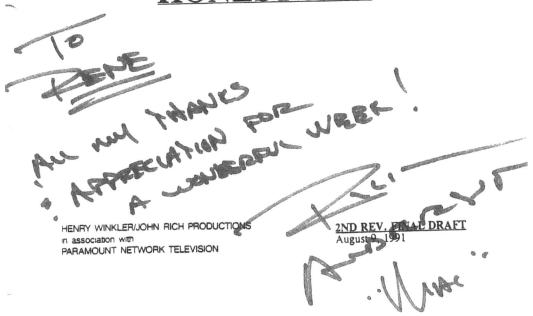

HENRY WINKLER/JOHN RICH PRODUCTIONS
in association with
PARAMOUNT NETWORK TELEVISION

2ND REV. FINAL DRAFT
August 9, 1991

NETWORK TELEVISION

MacGyver

Richard Dean Anderson

Medical Center (1969)

Starring Chad Everett
Behind the Scenes

I got a call from my agent to try out for a part on a new TV series called *Medical Center*. The series was starring a great actor, Chad Everett. Boy, if I could just get the part, I would be playing a young doctor on the show. The show was about young doctors and the adventures of medicine and curing the patients.

I had been on casting calls before, and usually, about fifty to one hundred young men would try out. It was really hard. You had to look good, be the right height and weight, and have a good attitude and smile. A couple of days later, I got the call. I got the job! I was to be a young doctor on the series. I was so excited.

On my first day, they had me made up as a doctor, and what I had to do was be in the title shots of the beginning of the show. The shot began of an ambulance going down the highway to the hospital as the camera followed the ambulance. The screen opened up on the right side of the TV, and a doctor appeared to be looking in a microscope and writing notes. That was me. The camera opened to three more young doctors on the screen.

I did that for five years. Chad Everett was known as Dr. Joe Gannon, and I was the doctor assistant in the operating room. Well, being on the series for five years, you become like family. So Chad and I became real good friends. Things the public did not know about Chad was, he was a prankster. He would tell funny jokes and pull pranks on the show while filming. One of my favorite ones was, he had me get a lot of spaghetti and hide it in the operating room in the dummy we were to operate on. I was a little leery about this. I did not want to get into trouble. Chad assured me to not to worry; he was the star, and there would be no trouble for me. Okay, I was game to go along with this.

The director said action. Chad said to me, "Scalpel." I handed him the scalpel. He cut the dummy open. Everyone was so quiet and serious as Dr. Joe Gannon was opening up the chest of the dummy. He pulled some spaghetti out and put it on my plate and pulled more. Now the Director was wondering, *What the hell, this is not in the script.*

As Chad pulled out the rest of the spaghetti from the patient, no one could stop laughing. It took over half an hour to get back to work. The entire crew was laughing so hard, but Chad got the most fun out of it. He said to me, "See, everybody needs a good laugh."

After another half hour, the director told us we had to get back to work. "Let's make this serious. I don't want the patient to die." Ha ha. Boy, I thought I was in trouble, but I was not. Probably thanks to Chad.

Another funny one was when he had guests come to the show to watch. There was this fake elevator in the hospital hall, and he would have his guest sit next to the elevator. Then he would get about fifty people to go around the back of the elevator and come in through a secret wall. Well, when the elevator doors opened up, people began to come out of the elevator and continued to keep coming out until there was no room in the hall. One guest said, "How big is that elevator?" We all had a good laugh.

Well, I was real sorry to see that series end in 1976, as we all were. So what do you do when a series ends? Well, we all say goodbye and start looking for a new job.

About thirty years later, I had developed and built new sets on my new movie ranch Blue Cloud. The ranch became extremely successful because I had built sets no other movie ranch or studio had built. I constructed a huge Afghanistan town. Hundreds of shows and TV series came to film. Some include *JAG*, *NCIS* with Mark Harmon, *Iron Man 1* and *2* with Robert Downey Jr., *American Sniper* with Bradley Cooper, and many more. I had Army camps, caves, gas stations, airplane hangar with a dirt runway, and a one hundred acres of movie sets. So you could see I was very busy.

I had a show filming one day, and I was talking to the FSA (fire safety adviser). There was always one on each show for fire safety. In drove a baby-blue Thunderbird looking like he was lost. I said to the FSA, "Oh my god, that is Chad Everett! I was on the *Medical Center* series with him."

He pulled up and said, "Where can I park?"

I told him, "Mr. Everett, you can park anywhere you want."

He said, "Are you sure?"

"I am sure as I own this movie ranch."

He got out of the car and said, "How the hell are you, Rene? I remember you. You were on my *Medical Center* series." Then he said, "You own this movie ranch?"

I said, "Yes, I do."

He then told me, "You had come a long way up the ladder."

I told him, "I had, but it was not real easy." He told me he was really proud of me.

The FSA was blown away after I told him the story of Chad and me. Chad and I got to talk about the good old times we had on his show. The show wrapped, and he said, "See you on the next one."

Well, sorry to say, I did not see him again. As time passed, we all got busy and did our own thing. On July 24, 2012, I heard my friend passed away. I will miss Chad, just knowing he is not here anymore. But I still have my memories.

The Untouchables

Starring Robert Stack
Behind the Scenes
Short Stories

This was a great series to work on. Robert Stack was great to work with. I usually played an Italian person. Sometimes I played an FBI agent or a newspaper boy and usually was killed in the scene. One time, I remember very well I played a delivery boy delivering flowers to an office. I was dressed as a delivery boy with dark-brown curly hair and lots of makeup on. In the old days, they used a lot of makeup because the film was in black and white. My job was to deliver flowers to an office. The flowers were on a cart with a bomb in the flowers. They had rigged me with a hidden harness, so as I pushed the flowers into the office, they set off the bomb and yanked me through the door on a mat while the bomb blast broke the door, with fire, flame, and sugar glass flying out on me. Great scene, cut, and print. I always loved to hear the words "Print it," then I knew it was a done deal and I never had to do that again. Of course, I was sore for a week after doing something like that.

Now came the easy part—the close-ups. They had to be absolutely perfect, with many takes and different angles. Now I did not plan on this; for the rest of the day, it was on me. Then came the makeup man with a gallon of blood. Of course, it was not real blood but a gallon of Hershey's chocolate. They proceeded to pour it all over me; after all, I had been blown up. Now they were ready to roll.

"Rene, get ready."

I called, "Ready." And the makeup man poured a mouthful of chocolate in my mouth. When action was called, I was to let it ooze out of my mouth. Oh my god, this went on all day, take after take.

When we wrapped, they said, "Good job, Rene, so get a shower and clean up."

Robert Stack said, "Thank you."

To this day, I can barely stand to eat chocolate. I wonder why. Well, that's show business.

Don Knotts

Behind the Scenes

One of the greatest funny comedian I ever got to know was Don Knotts. I had the great privilege to work with him. I was hired to stunt double him and do his rehearsals while he watched. He could not stand on his feet very long, so I did all the moves, dialogue, everything he did in the film. I did it at least three to four times for him. Yes, that meant kissing the girls in the movies. Wow, what a job! And they paid me very well too. After all, Don Knotts liked me. I was told, "Do your job and don't bug him. You are to be seen and not heard." He had me doing a lot of his personal business on the show also.

In 1968, I was on his movie *The Shakiest Gun in the West*. That was a funny one and right up my alley because it was a Western and I am a cowboy. He did not like horses. He had me do all his horse work. One funny scene was, he was supposed to ride a big, tall Clydesdale horse dressed like an Indian squaw. To get on the horse, the joke was a five-foot rope ladder to climb up on. So they dressed me up to look like an Indian squaw to double him. He was glad for me to do it so he did not have to. You just never know what you are going to do in this crazy business.

The other movie I was on with Don Knotts was *The Love God?* in 1969. That was a whole different type of movie. He played a sex symbol, and all the women chased him. I had a ball rehearsing for him, always around the most beautiful, gorgeous women in the world. Don told me I was having too much fun. We laughed, and I told him I always wanted to work with him on *The Andy Griffith Show*.

He said, "Really?" He asked me, "Why did you not come over and introduce yourself?"

I told him I really did not want to bother him, and I was just happy to be working with him now. He told me he appreciated my loyalty and all I had done to help him, and he appreciated working with me.

Well, we went on and finished the show, had a wrap party, said farewell and "See you on the next one." That's show business.

Stars Earn Stripes (2012)

Starring Todd Palin
Behind the Scenes

I got the contract to do an episode of *Stars Earn Stripes*, a reality Army game show where they were to fire live ammunition, Army helicopters, bombs, explosions, Hummers, and lots of smoke. I had plenty of room at my Blue Cloud Movie Ranch, consisting of approximately one hundred acres. They chose my ranch because I had the location they wanted.

My back lot was designed to look like you were in Afghanistan with room for Army helicopters to fly in and make their bomb runs and be movie safe. One-half of the ranch was used for crew trailers, parking, honey wagons, special effects, and so on. They had guards and a full medical team ready for any situation.

As I was looking at the call sheet to see who was the guest star contestants, I saw the name Todd Palin as one of the contestants. Now I got really excited as I was a huge fan of his wife, Sarah Palin. Oh, boy, I had to meet him. So I waited at his star wagon dressing room for him to show up from filming. Finally, the limo pulled up, and Todd got out dressed in his Army clothes. He looked like he had been through a war (well, a fake one). I introduced myself. He was very nice and polite. I asked him if Sarah Palin was coming to see him. He said he did not know, but there was a possibility she would come to see him tomorrow. I asked if he knew where she was. He asked why I wanted to know. I told him I purchased her book and thought maybe I could get her to autograph it for me. He told me he was sorry but he did not know her schedule. We talked a minute more, and then he needed to clean up and get the dust, makeup, and bomb residue off. He really did look like a mess. He had to be a nice guy to stand and talk to me as long as he did. Well, just a bummer, I really wanted to meet Sarah Palin.

Well, a couple of months went by, and while I was in a grocery store, I picked up a magazine on my way home. At every signal, I glanced at the magazine, and on the back page, I could not believe what I saw. Sarah Palin was scheduled to be at the Oak Tree Gun Club on Saturday for a book signing. *That's tomorrow! Oh my god, I am going to be there and bring my book to have her sign it.*

The next day at 6:00 a.m., I was in line waiting for her. Three hours later, three black SUV limos pulled in. Now over one thousand people were waiting, and I was about fiftieth in line.

As two limos unloaded with security guards like I had never seen before, they opened the SUV door for her limo, and Sarah Palin got out and was immediately surrounded by her guards and escorted into the building. I said, "Wow, what a show." As people were entering the building to see her, they got thirty seconds to say hello and have her sign their book. Wow, not much time to see her, but I had a plan to see her longer.

As my time approached, I started to smile at her, and she smiled back. When my turn came, I handed her my book and told her that her husband, Todd, was just at my movie ranch filming his TV reality show. She asked my name, and I told her Rene Veluzat. She said to the cameraman for him to take our picture. Wow! I thanked her. As I was leaving, she called me by name and asked how Todd did on the contest. I told her he did fantastic. Sarah replied, "Great." What an exciting two minutes I had with Sarah Palin.

Rene and Sarah Palin

BOOK SIGNING

SWEET
Freedom
A DEVOTIONAL

SARAH
PALIN

Saturday December 5th, 2015
11:00AM to 1:30PM
No Personal Photography
*Pictures will be taken by a Professional Photographer and will be available for free!
Books will be available for Purchase.

23121 Coltrane Ave Newhall, CA 91321
WWW.OAKTREEGUNCLUB.COM 661-259-7441

Oak Tree Gun Club

157

Johnny Depp

Behind the Scenes

I was on a movie with Johnny Depp called *Don Juan DeMarco* at my movie ranch in the Mexican town. This was a difficult show to negotiate because of Johnny Depp and Marlon Brando. Now I knew Marlon Brando from the movie I worked called *The Chase*. I didn't think there would be a problem with Marlon, but I was not so sure about Johnny Depp.

Boy, was I fooled when I met Johnny. He was the nicest, polite actor I ever met. We hit it off right away. I made sure that Johnny's star wagon dressing room was placed on the best location on the ranch. I put the star wagon dressing room under a large oak tree for shade and made sure the water truck sprayed water around his dressing room trailer for dust and to cool off the dirt, as it was very hot when the movie was shot.

Everything was going just great when Johnny would show up on the set. I would always open his limo door for him. We would greet each other, and we became good friends. A couple of days later of the shooting, the limo driver would pick up Johnny from his dressing room and drive him one block to the set. On the way to the set, if he saw me, he would stop the limo and pick me up to ride to the set with him.

The assistant director called on the radio, "Where is Johnny? We are losing the light. He is putting us in the toilet." The limo driver's walkie-talkie was on, and we heard this as Johnny laughed. Somebody came on the radio and advised he stopped to pick up a guy named Rene. The radio went dead silent.

"That is the guy who owns the movie ranch, and Johnny likes him."

The guy on the radio said, "Okay, no problem."

As the limo arrived on the Mexican set and Johnny got out, about one hundred Mexican town people greeted him. The director was now very upset about this and yelled, "We do not have time for this! We have to get the shot. Get Johnny in."

Johnny stopped and said, "Wait a minute, these are my fans and the people who goes to the movies to see me." So Johnny took twenty minutes to sign autographs and pictures.

The director saw what was happening and backed off and waited until Johnny was done. The director then asked Johnny, "Mr. Depp, are you ready?" Johnny said he was.

As Johnny took his position for the scene on the water fountain for the sword fight scene, the director called, "Action, Johnny." Johnny starts sword fighting as three cameras were rolling for about four minutes of action until the director called, "Cut! Beautiful, Johnny, great. You are now done for the day."

Wow, what a day's work—four minutes. Johnny and I got back into the limo to take Johnny back to his dressing room so he could change and go home.

As Johnny was leaving, he said, "Rene, be my guest, hang out in my dressing room."

"Thanks, Johnny. I will see you tomorrow." *Wow,* I thought, *that is great. He is allowing me to hang out in his big beautiful dressing room. Why not? The worst that can happen would be all the crew and 399 drivers would be jealous of me. So what? He said I can be his guest.* So inside I went. I could not believe how beautiful it was inside. He had decorated it Ali Baba–style, red drapes all over with all kinds of plush red pillows, really thick red carpet, and to top it off, anything you could want to drink and about one hundred red candles. A half hour was all I could take of this atmosphere. I decided I had to leave before I got spoiled and wanted a star wagon like that for myself.

The next day, when Johnny came to the movie ranch, he seemed to like just hanging out with the crew, just like a regular guy. He even cooked dinner for the crew—the best mahi-mahi I ever tasted. The show went super great for me, and to top it off, I was invited to the next location to have lunch with Marlon Brando. I regretted I did not take time off to have lunch with Marlon Brando.

Best Family Shows

Behind the Scenes

I always loved working on family shows; there were no killings, no blowup scenes, and no fights. Just go to work and double your favorite character on *Leave It to Beaver*. Yes, I go way back to the '50s. Tony Dow, the star, and I would go to lunch in my Corvette and cruise Bob's Big Boy in Toluca Lake. We got the greatest kid out of this. Girls would yell and scream and follow us back to the studio.

The show *My Three Sons*, starring Don Grady and Fred MacMurray, was also a great show to work. I always rehearsed for Don Grady, and I was his double. Every time he did a guest appearance on other shows, I went with him. One exciting show where I was his double was *Have Gun—Will Travel*, starring Richard Boone. Don played a young Indian boy, so I would double him riding a horse in the mountains of Lone Pine, California.

One of my big favorites was *The Adventures of Ozzie and Harriet* show. I was Ricky Nelson's friend, his malt shop buddy, his fraternity brother, and dancer on the show. We all had so much fun on *The Adventures of Ozzie and Harriet* show, dancing to Ricky Nelson's music. Where could you work, be with the stars and dance all day, and then get paid for it? What a job and what a life. But all good stuff is not without problems. To be on the show, you had to be clean-shaven and with a very, very short haircut. But to work on the Westerns, I had to have long hair and three to four days of whiskers. So I had to figure that out. I bought a long hair wig to wear on the Westerns. No one figured I was wearing a wig, so I got away with it. Thank God I bought a good one; it never fell off. Ha ha.

Another funny and fun show I worked on was *The Munsters*, with Yvonne de Carlo, Fred Gwynne, and Al Lewis. I usually rehearsed the scenes for Grandpa, Al Lewis, and Fred Gwynne, the munster. It was always hot in his munster suit, so because he was so tall, they had made him a special munster chair. And because the munster suit was so hot and he could not take it off all the time, they rigged his suit for air-conditioning. This was an air compressor with an air hose he put down his shirt. That did the job. After every take, he ran for the chair, and his assistant fired up the air compressor to cool him off. The munster, Fred Gwynne, told me he was so happy at the end of the day to take the suit and makeup off and go home and relax. It was a great show and a fun one to work on. I really enjoyed working on these shows.

Another show I worked on was in 1957, *Bachelor Father*, starring John Forsythe, Noreen Corcoran, and Sammee Tong. Can you imagine I was called in to rehearse for Sammy Tong? We worked very closely, getting his moves marked on the spot where he was going to act and do dialogue. When I met John Forsythe and he found out I liked racehorses, he wanted me to stay on the show.

As we were talking in between shots, I told him my dad and I owned racehorses and ran them at Santa Anita and Hollywood Park Racetracks and that Willie Shoemaker was our jockey. He could not believe this. He loved racehorses and told me he goes to the racetrack every chance he gets. He liked betting on the horses. So after some days later, my dad and I were at Santa Anita, sitting in our box seats, waiting for our race to come up. When it did come up, we won the race and were so excited. At the same time, I heard from the box seat next to us, "Congratulations, Rene, for winning the race. I bet on your horse." It was John Forsythe.

My dad and I owned a lot of racehorses and were very successful. I had my dad, in 1963, buy a Silver Spur Rolls-Royce, and I was his chauffeur, driving my dad in that Rolls-Royce to all the racetracks and pulling up to all the other Rolls and watching the stars get out of them, especially Lou Costello. I took my chauffeur's hat off, threw it in the back seat, and then became one of the owner of a racehorse, as we walked into the racetrack along with all the other owners, trainers, and movie stars. Dad and I had so much fun.

So after fifteen years of driving my dad to and from the racetrack and special events, I asked Dad if I could have the Rolls when he retired and I carried on. He said, "Of course, you can." I was so happy, and we had so many good and fond memories in that car. Sadly, my dad passed away on April 9, 2000, at the age of 101 years. Unfortunately, even though my dad promised me the car, it was not to be. My two brothers went to his house and took the Silver Spur Rolls-Royce from his garage.

Even though I had signed and notarized papers stating I was to have the car, I could not get possession of it. I was totally crushed, and I am still upset about it today. My brothers may have the car, but I have the memories.

I believe in karma—what comes around goes around. I believe in karma so much that a miracle in my books happened. I got a call from a French businessman asking if I was interested in buying a Rolls-Royce from a prince in Saudi Arabia. I could not believe this. I bought the Rolls-Royce from the prince. Now is that not good karma?

You know, in life, you always want what you worked for and what you achieved. I had a jockey suit made especially for Willie Shoemaker while he was racing our horses. It was red and gold with Diamond V on the back. I also lost this along with my saddle, bridles, and tack and other accessories when my dad passed away. All my personal belonging disappeared when I went to collect them after my dad passed away. I am still waiting for the karma to come around.

The beautiful brown Rolls-Royce is on the cover of my book. It is not only a beautiful Rolls-Royce, it came from a prince in Saudi Arabia. So yes, I am very fortunate and lucky. I do believe in karma.

Rene doubling Don Grady

CHAPTER 7

War Dogs—PSA Charity

Behind the Scenes

I DO A lot of charity work at my movie ranch, especially for Paws for Pets, who provide dogs to military veterans. The K9 dogs come from Afghanistan, who were in the war and were left there. They bring them back to the United States and connect them to war veterans in need.

So I was contacted by Lorry of Paws for Pets to do a PSA charity commercial in my Afghanistan town involving K9 dogs. They had no money; it was just for charity. So Lorry, the location person, told me she was at a heavy metal concert to see Rob Zombie, and after the concert, she asked him to donate something for the War Dogs. He said he would love to as he loved dogs. He said he had a special guitar that he could autograph and donate. He also had his band members add their autographs. He was thrilled to do it.

Now Lorry told me all she had for the location fee was Rob Zombie's autographed guitar. I told her I would be honored to do their show and take the guitar in lieu of a location fee. I was excited to get Rob Zombie's guitar to put with all my other memorabilia I had from the other shows I had done. I had my *Planet of the Apes* mask I wore in the original *Planet of the Apes* movie starring Charlton Heston. The guitar next to the mask would be perfect for my office.

I knew Rob Zombie was very famous. He made four studio albums and was the founding member of the heavy metal band White Zombie. He had produced, directed, and written twenty-seven movies, including one called *House of 1,000 Corpses*, a 2003 American horror film, also coscored by Rob Zombie. This was his first film in his directorial debut and the first film series. This is unbelievable! He did that show, *House of 1,000 Corpses*, at my movie ranch, and I coordinated for him.

Small world, isn't it? So all I had to do for the PSA charity War Dogs and to get the famous guitar was to give them my movie ranch for a day to film anywhere they wanted. For example, that included the movie ranch for twelve hours in the Afghanistan town, where we filmed *Iron Man*, *American Sniper*, and tons of other shows, including the TV shows *JAG* and *NCIS* with Mark Harmon. It also included the Army camp, seven Hummers, one Army tank, six-by-six Army cargo trucks, sixteen Army tents and numerous Army props, one Huey helicopter, four-thousand-gallon water truck for fire protection, site rep fees, and my management fees. Wow! They got a ten-thousand-dollar deal for charity. I was happy to do this once in a while.

The day when they moved in came, and they were now very happy. In the meantime, I told my son, Marcel, he was going to be the location manager for the ranch on this show. He asked who was in the show. I told him he would not know them as they were dogs and we were doing it for charity.

"They are giving me a guitar from some guy named Rob Zombie. Who the hell is this guy?" I was just kidding, but Marcel did not know I was kidding.

Marcel said, "Dad, you are nuts! Rob Zombie is the most famous person in the world. Is he coming to the ranch?"

I told him, "No, but his guitar is. That is what they are giving me in lieu of location fees."

"Oh, I see," he said.

So the show was going very well about now, and I asked the location lady, Lorry, if she had my location fees (the guitar). She responded, "Oh, didn't Marcel tell you? He met me at the gate early this morning and got the location fees, your guitar. He is such a nice boy!"

So I went to find Marcel to find out where the guitar was. He said, "Dad, I didn't think you really wanted the guitar. You don't even know who the guy is."

I told him that was just a joke, that I way playing on him. "Give me the guitar."

He said, "Dad, please let me have the guitar to put next to the basketball you got me from Shaquille O'Neal."

"Well, okay." I caved in. He was so excited to get the guitar.

War Dogs was done filming. It was a good day, and everybody thanked me. Marcel got the famous guitar, and I got great satisfaction from doing the charity work.

War Dogs—PSA Charity

Behind The Scenes

I do a lot of charity work at my Movie Ranch, especially for Paws For Pets, who provide dogs to military veterans. The K-9 dogs come from Afghanistan, who were in the war and were left there. They bring them back to the United States and connect them to war veterans in need.

So, I was contacted by Larry of Paws For Pets to do a P.S.A charity commercial in my Afghanistan Town involving K-9 dogs. They have no money; it is just for charity. So Lorry, the location person told me he was at a heavy metal concert to see Rob Zombie in concert and after the concert, he asked him to donate something for the War Dogs. He said he would love to as he loves dogs. He said he had a special guitar that he could autograph and donate. He also had his band members add their autographs. He was thrilled to do it.

Now Lorry tells me all she has for the location fee is the Rob Zombie's autographed guitar. I told her I would be honored to do your show and take the guitar in lieu of a location fee. I am excited to get Rob Zombie's guitar to put with all my other memorabilia I have from the other shows I have done. I have my "Planet of The Apes" mask I wore in the original "Planet of The Apes" movie starring Charlton Heston. The guitar next to the mask will be perfect for my office.

I know Rob Zombie is very famous. He made four studio albums and is the founding member of the heavy metal band "White Zombie". He has produced, directed and written 27 movies; including one called "House of a Thousand Corpses", a 2003 American Horror film written, co-scored and directed by Rob Zombie. This is his first film in his directorial debut and the first film series. This is unbelievable! He did that show "House of a Thousand Corpses" at my Movie Ranch and I coordinated for him.

Small world isn't it! So, all I have to do for P.S.A. charity, "War Dogs" and get the famous guitar is to give them my Movie Ranch for a day to film anywhere they want. For example that includes the movie ranch for twelve hours in the Afghanistan Town where we filmed "Iron Man", "American Sniper" and tons of other shows including the TV shows "Jag", "NCIS" with Mark Harmon. It also includes the Army Camp, 7 Hummers, 1 Army Tank, 6X6 Army cargo trucks, 16 Army tents and numerous Army props; 1 Huey helicopter, 14,000 gallon water truck for fire protection, site rep fees and my management fees. Wow!! They got a $10,000.00 deal for charity. I am happy to do this once in a while.

CHAPTER 8

Area 51

Behind the Scenes

I DID A lot of Roswell and Area 51 shows for the History Channel. Some parts of my movie ranch looked like Roswell, where supposedly the UFO crashed.

One Area 51 show seemed to be different than all the rest of the shows I did. This show came to the set, but the prop guy actually forgot the star of the show—the alien mannequins. So he went into a panic and asked me if I had an alien.

"Are you kidding? I don't have any aliens." But now I have two aliens in my garage sitting on my Harley-Davidson. So I advised him to go to a party or joke store to see if they had any blow-up dolls.

He left in a hurry. The studio still did not know he forgot the alien dolls. He came back and said to me, "Thanks for your advice. I got two aliens."

As he took them out of the box and blew them up with air, I asked him, "What the hell are these?"

"I got these two beautiful women dolls in a sex store. They are going to be my two aliens." Then he blew them up and spray-painted their faces gray and used some weird makeup, then he put them on a stretcher and covered them up to their necks. "Well, here you are, two aliens."

I could not believe how inventive this studio prop guy was. He showed them to the director, and he said, "They look great. Take them to the set where the UFO crash site is."

He laid them on the ground around the UFO crashed spaceship made up of a lot of aluminum foil all over the ground. They did the scene at night, and that made it eerier when the soldiers picked them up and put them on a stretcher and then into an Army cargo truck. The truck was one of my good Army cargo trucks. Then they caravanned them to an abandoned airplane hangar somewhere in my Area 51 set. The scene was, they unloaded the aliens, carried the stretcher, and put them in the airplane hangar. Then a tall scientist came over to examine the alien bodies. The scene looked great. The director was happy.

In the meantime, this scientist guy, the actor, tall, thin-faced, wearing thick black reading glasses, with a white doctor's long coat on, kept eyeballing me, like he wanted to talk to me. So I went over and introduced myself and told him I was the owner of this movie ranch. He introduced himself as Bob Lazar. This guy, Bob Lazar, said he thought my movie ranch was right on with the Roswell aliens' UFO crash site and the airplane hangar. We talked for quite some time as I listened intensively. He told me stories that he worked at Area 51, told me he worked with the aliens there with the UFO spaceships they had to figure out how they fly. He also told me he worked around real aliens and had been in and around the UFO craft. He told me they were real.

I finally asked the director who this guy, Bob Lazar, was. "He talked my leg off about UFOs and aliens. He seems to know a lot, or is he just blowing smoke?"

The director told me, "He is the real guy that worked at the real Area 51. He knows what is really going on, and I believe him."

Wow! I was talking to the real deal, Bob Lazar, personally. I always believed in UFOs and aliens, and now that had just put the icing on the cake.

Years before this show, I was building an Army camp set in a canyon, kinda like the MASH set on that TV series. It was about 7:00 a.m., and I was with my construction crew working on building the Army sets. We had two generators running. It was real foggy that morning, and the fog was very thick. I could not even see the top of the hills. As we were working, we heard a real loud boom. Everybody got panicked. I said, "No worries, it is just the space shuttle coming back from a space trip." Everyone was relieved. Just seconds later, we heard a very loud screeching noise. I thought it was one of my generators, so I shut it off. The screeching got louder, so I shut off my other generator. Now it was totally quiet, no noise, no screeching. Just then, the screeching started again and got louder. It traveled in circles in split second. We all huddled up, scared. *What the hell is making such a loud screeching noise?*

We were just about to get in our trucks and make a run for it. Then the screeching noise stopped. Finally, my shaken-up crew and I cautiously went back to work. We did not hear the noise anymore. We finished building the Army camp, and everything was good. Anytime I went into the Army camp or did a show there, I always worried if the screeching noise would come back.

Several years later, I heard at my Rotary Club dinner meeting that there was to be a retired Army colonel from Roswell, New Mexico, to be our guest speaker. "This is great. I am definitely going to be there Tuesday night at the Rotary Club meeting." This was good. It was always held at a fancy steak restaurant in Toluca Lake, California. We could be more relaxed, have a great steak and a glass of red wine, and enjoy the meeting.

After dinner, our guest speaker was introduced. He said he was retired and declassified, and he was going to tell us a story about a UFO that crashed in Roswell, New Mexico. What he told us made our hair stand straight up. Yes, indeed, a UFO did crash, and there were three aliens recovered—two were dead and one was alive. They were all taken back to Area 51, and all the spacecraft and pieces were taken back to Area 51 also.

The retired Army colonel said he personally observed all this and was at the crash site. Almost everything he told us we, at one time or another, had filmed on the History Channel show. I filmed about twenty episodes of Area 51 for the History Channel. He talked for about an hour. You could hear a pin drop when he was talking.

After his speech, he asked the Rotary members if they had any sightings or something they had heard. And then I said yes and stood up and introduced myself. I told him about the foggy morning my crew and I heard the loud screeching all around us upon our space shuttle returning to Earth. I asked him, "What do you think it was?"

He said, "A shocker." He said he thought a UFO followed our space shuttle back to Earth and was circling overhead where we were working.

"Okay, thank you for your answer. I thought that for years. Now after hearing your speech and the answer you gave me, I believe it. Wow! After all these years, I finally got an answer to my belief. Thank you, Colonel."

Rene with Area 51 aliens

Rene with Area 51 aliens

Rene with Area 51 aliens

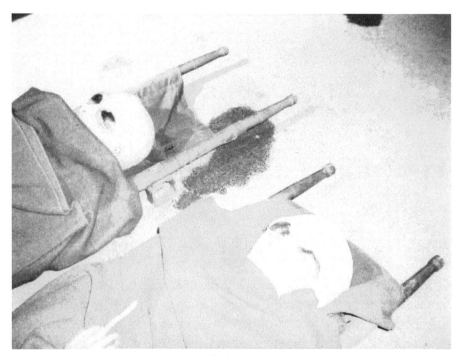

Rene with Area 51 aliens

Rene and the Area 51 flying saucer

CHAPTER 9

On a Funny Note—the Foot

Behind the Scenes

ON ANOTHER SCOUT day, just like the girl scouting the cave, another lady called me and wanted to scout a riverbed. Great, I got one. She came out to the ranch. I put her in my scout truck, and we went up the canyon at the ranch to look at the riverbed. As we were driving to the riverbed, she said, "Let's get out here and walk down to the riverbed so I can take pictures as we go along."

Everything was going good. She was happy taking pictures as she said, "I think this will work." She tripped on something and almost fell down. As I caught her from falling, we both looked down to see what she tripped on. Something looked weird protruding out of the sand. As I started to dig whatever it was, she said, "That's all right. Let's go." If you knew me, I would want to know what it was. I dug the thing up as she looked on, and I uncovered a foot that had apparently been severed from the body, kind of rotten and torn from a leg. Well, she screamed as I picked up the gruesome foot.

Then I realized it was a rubber foot. I was thinking a mile a minute to figure out what the hell. I then remembered as I was calming the lady location manager down that it was from a show we did where they blew up a helicopter in the air and the helicopter crashed there. I explained to her that they cleaned up the fake crash scene and apparently forgot to pick up the ankle and foot from the dummy helicopter pilot.

Now she believed me that it was not a scene of a vicious murder. She then laughed and said she would still rent the ranch.

I said, "Great. I am wondering if they got all the dummy body parts from here."

She said, "Very funny."

On a Funnier Note—The Cave

Behind the Scenes

It was a beautiful day for location scouting. I got a call from a lady location manager wanting to scout my cave set for a show. I waited and waited, and she finally showed up. All was forgiven; after all, I wanted her to rent the cave set. Always before any location person showed up, I prechecked the location, in this case, the cave. I always checked to see if there were any rattlesnakes, coyotes, bugs, or anything else that would be bad. Everything was good.

So I approached the cave to go in, and I said I needed to check the cave for mountain lions, snakes, or any other critters. She was late for her appointment, and something could have gone into the cave while I was waiting for her to arrive. I told her to wait outside while I checked. I went into the cave and got about thirty feet in the cave, and unbeknownst to me, she was right behind me. Just then, a bird came flying right by me. Again, I was not aware she was right behind me. She screamed. Not knowing what it was, she grabbed me from behind and scared the shit out of me. Not knowing she was behind me, we both landed on the floor of the dark cave.

As we scrambled to get up, the bird flew out, and we both ran out of the cave. She said she was sorry. I said okay, and we both composed ourselves. I got her a flashlight, and then we both scouted the cave. She did decide to rent the cave set for her show.

Wayne Newton

Behind the Scenes

One of my favorite singers while I was growing up was Wayne Newton. I listened to his songs every chance I got. My favorites are "Danke Schoen" and "Daddy, Don't You Walk So Fast."

The fun part of this story was that later in life, I looked similar to Wayne. So while at my movie ranch Blue Cloud, people would say, "Who is that guy, the owner?"

"Oh, you will know him. He looks just like Wayne Newton."

I had a lot of fun being Wayne Newton's double. When my wife Patti and I went to Vegas for fun, everywhere I went, people would ask me for my autograph. A tour bus would be driving down Las Vegas Boulevard, and the tour guide would stop the bus and say, "This is your lucky day, folks. There is Wayne Newton going into that hotel." So sixty to one hundred people followed me into the hotel. Yes, I did sign autographs as "Rene, Wayne Newton' movie photo double." I did not want to disappoint them. They were happy taking picture of them and me.

Another funny episode in the saga of Rene Veluzat was that my wife, Patti, took me to one of her business parties. It was a Hollywood star–impersonating party. We were supposed to dress up as our favorite stars. Patti dressed up like Lucille Ball and asked me to dress like Ricky Ricardo. I said no, I did not want to dress up but I would just wear my black tux.

Okay, when we got to the party, we walked the red carpet into the hotel. Everybody was dressed up as their favorite star. It was a contest to see who had the best costume. As we were enjoying this great Hollywood star–impersonating party, the announcer came on stage and said he wanted the audience to pick the winner.

"Okay, all you ladies come on stage and let the audience pick the winner." As the announcer walked by each person, he put his hand on their head, and the audience would clap. When he got to Patti, dressed as Lucille Ball, the audience unanimously tore the house down with clapping. Patti won the contest as Lucy.

Then the announcer asked for all the men to come on stage. All the men got on stage. The announcer then said, "I think we missed one." Everybody looked around, including me. The announcer looked at me and said, "You, sir, Wayne Newton."

I said, "Oh no, it is for all of you. I did not dress up."

The announcer stepped off the stage and walked to my table and put his hand on my head. The audience again tore the house down with clapping and singing "Danke Schoen." The announcer said, "We have another winner, Wayne Newton."

I could not believe this. I stood up with my martini and said, "Thank you. *Danke schoen.*"

Patti said, "I can't believe this either. For your birthday in December, I am taking you to see the Wayne Newton show!"

So in December, we were at the Wayne Newton show, front-row center seats. Wayne came on stage singing and greeting people, shaking their hands. As he approached me, the spotlight came on me, and Wayne Newton did a double take. He could not believe this person looked like him. "Am I looking at a mirror?"

I said, "Hi, Wayne, I am your cousin." He took a gasp of air, and I said, "Just kidding. I have been your photo double for years."

Wayne said, "Well, thank you very much. Keep up the good work." He laughed and asked my name.

I told him, "Rene Veluzat."

And he asked the audience, "Give Rene a hand. And thank you again. Enjoy the show."

I really enjoyed the show. I even won some money and had a great birthday thanks to my wife, Patti.

Rene Veluzat, aka Wayne Newton

CHAPTER 10

Western Shows

The Long Ride Home

Starring Randy Travis, Eric Roberts, Ernest Borgnine, Vaughn Taylor,
Paul Tinder, Garry Marshall, Jerry Doyle, and Stella Stevens
Directed by Robert Marcarelli
Behind the Scenes of Producing a Movie

IN THE YEAR 2000, I got an opportunity to produce a Western called *The Long Ride Home*. I was glad I did, and I won a Telly Award for producing *The Long Ride Home*. It was a beautiful trophy. Besides my producing duties, I built all the Western set at my ranch and spent two weeks at a Western town in Malibu Creek State Park, along with being at all the meetings. I was very happy with all the actors we cast for the show, especially Ernie Borgnine, who was my friend from the series *McHale's Navy* in 1962 and *Airwolf* with Jan-Michael Vincent in 1984. I had been a stunt double for Jan-Michael Vincent in the *Airwolf* series. I was especially awaiting to meet Eric Roberts. I was told not to bother him on the set because he was always in deep thought about the movie.

After being on the set for three weeks, I finally met the great guy and actor. We talked briefly here and there about my ranch and what was shot there.

So this was funny. A couple of days after, we had a light shooting schedule, and it seemed everybody was in a good mood that day. The makeup artist girl said, "Let's take some photos." So everyone was taking photos, and I got into it.

I asked Eric for a picture, and he responded, "Sure, li'l buddy. Get in here." He asked a fellow crew member to take our picture on the count of three. He had his arm on my shoulder and said, "One, two, three." As they snapped the picture on three, he kissed me on the cheek. I was so shocked, and everyone laughed so hard, including Eric Roberts. I laughed too. Eric said, "Let's do another one." Okay, he did the same thing, and the crew laughed even harder. You know, it was all right with me. I was the producer, and it broke a lot of tension on the set. Well, doing a Western was not easy. Eric said, "Let's do it again."

"Okay," I said, "but no kissing this time." I got the picture, and we all laughed as we went back to work.

Randy Travis—the first day at the Western town for Randy Travis, we were all looking for him. "Where is he?"

"He is still in the hotel in Beverly Hills waiting for his limo." The driver got lost, and we finally had to send a production assistant to get him. Little did we know what was going on. The assistant production man called and said he had him and his wife and were on their way. We were all relieved.

We eagerly waited for them to show up. Then they came, and we were shocked when Randy and his wife got out of a little Toyota—beat up, dirty, with trash falling off the car. All we could do was apologize.

Randy, being a cowboy gentleman, said, "No problem."

I told the production crew this should never happen again. If the driver in the limo did not show up again, I would personally take them back to Beverly Hills in my new Lincoln Navigator. Sure enough, Randy was done for the day, and no limo driver showed up. So I was told, "Rene, get to the set. You are to take Randy and his wife to dinner and home."

"Oh, boy, no problem."

I loaded Randy and his wife in my Navigator, and we left the set. I told Randy that I was instructed to take them to dinner, to anyplace they wanted. I had the show's credit card.

Now I was thinking of a great restaurant in Beverly Hills and having a great evening with Randy Travis. As we were driving along, Randy said to his wife, "Liz, is that one of the restaurants we have back home?"

Liz said, "Yes, let's get food there."

"Rene, go back."

"You mean that hamburger place?"

"Yes, it is. Okay, that is what we want to eat."

Boy, was I disappointed. No great evening, just hamburgers in a hamburger drive-in. "Well, okay."

As we went through the drive-up line, they ordered. I decided not to order as I was now the limo driver driving with very important cargo. As we pulled up to the window, Randy reached out for his hamburger combos, and the cashier said, "Oh my god, it is Randy Travis!" And he dropped all the food on the ground. Randy said he would get it.

I said, "No, Randy, he will make it over again." He did, and we left. I got Randy home. What a day!

The next day, Randy Travis's million-dollar bus arrived from New Mexico to the ranch. He asked me if it would be okay if they could just stay on his bus at the ranch for the rest of the show.

I said, "Of course, that would be okay for me." No more worrying about taking him back to Beverly Hills, only to be presented a new situation. I ordered a guard to guard his million-dollar bus 24-7 until the movie was done and the bus left. Everything was going good. Who knew what was ahead?

Randy asked me if I knew where he could get some big spuds. I knew those were big potatoes.

"Yes," I told him, "I can help you get some." Well, I called the limo driver. I knew I should have just gotten the potatoes myself. But what trouble could you get into driving to Hollywood to the marketplace to get some big potatoes?

Well, six hours later, no limo driver, no potatoes. I called the driver over and over. Finally, he called and said, "Boss, I have some bad news."

I asked, "No potatoes?"

He said, "No, not that. I hit a car on the freeway, and the limo caught fire and burned down."

"What?" I couldn't believe it! It was true only in the movies. I rushed out and got Randy some big potatoes. He thanked me and did not know his limo got in a wreck and was burned down.

As I talked with Ernie Borgnine, he told me all he wanted was a case of water to drink.

"No problem, Ernie, I will take care of it."

Well, we finished the movie and had no more problems. This is one of the movies that I am proud of. Everyone, cast and crew, did a great job. And I am especially proud to have won a Telly Award for producing this movie.

Telly Award for Rene Veluzat, producer of *The Long Ride Home*

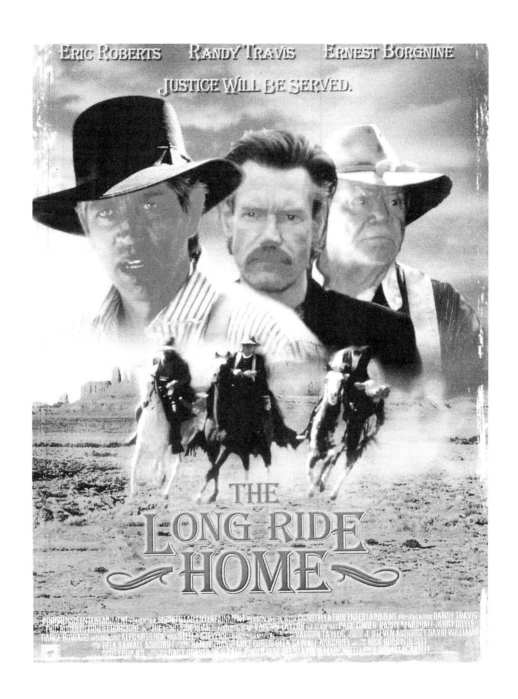

To,
René
My Thanks
Ernie
Borgnine

Ernest Borgnine and Rene Veluzat

Savate

Starring Olivier Gruner, James Brolin, Ian Ziering, and Ashley Laurence
A Western Action
Behind the Scenes

I had a stunt part playing the bartender. The part was that Olivier Gruner would beat me up. So for one week, every time Olivier saw me, he wanted to rehearse the part between us. After one week, I was so tired of rehearsing this part.

The day came to film this scene. I was in my bartender outfit, kinda looking like Kenny Rogers. He was in his Western outfit. The scene was for him to ask me for some information, but I would not tell him what he wanted to know. He grabbed me and yanked me over the bar top and choked me. Then he said, "I am not going to hurt you." Then he choked the crap out of me, but I still would not tell him. He then threw me over the bar as I took out all the glasses and whiskey bottles as I fell to the floor. That was the scene. That was the rehearsal; now we were ready to film it.

I had all my stunt pads on, and I was ready to go. The director said, "Roll three cameras." He called action, and Olivier started beating me up, socking me, and shaking the shit out of me. This was a lot more than we had rehearsed! Then he picked me up and threw me over the bar, as I took out more glasses and whiskey bottles. The director called, "Cut! Beautiful."

As I lay there behind the bar, it felt good for me. The director said, "Camera 1, are you good?"

Camera 1 said, "I did not roll."

"What? Camera 2, how was yours?"

"I did not roll either."

"What? Camera 3, tell me you rolled."

He said, "I am ready to roll when you are."

Then I said, "What the hell?"

Then you could hear a pin drop on the floor. Olivier yelled out, "That was the best one!" He was upset because it took a lot out of him and me to do the fight scene, which lasted three to four minutes.

The director came behind the bar as I was still lying there, trying to recover from the stunt and that no body rolled the camera. He got down on the floor next to my face and said he was sorry. But being in show business, he immediately said, "Rene, do you have another in you?" Of course, I knew he was going to say that, and he knew I would say, "Yes, I do have another one in me."

The stunt coordinator helped me up, readjusted my stunt pads, gave me a sip of water, and dusted me off, and we did the scene again. This time, all the cameras rolled, and this time, because we were doing it again, our adrenaline was high. We finished the scene, and the director was happy. I was done for the day. Oh well, that is show business.

Rene Veluzat as bartender in *Savate*

Wagon Train

Behind the Scenes

In the old days, in between jobs, I was tending bar at the famous one-hundred-year-old Saugus Café and Bar while waiting for a call from my agent for a job. I got a call to double the actor Michael Burns on a show called *Wagon Train*. That show ended my bartending career.

They liked me on *Wagon Train*, and I was doing all the riding stunts for the actor Michael Burns and also doing some bit parts in the show. For example, I was the first person to be seen sleeping with a woman on the show. I was very simply lying on the ground with my *Wagon Train* wife lying beside me; all our clothes and boots were on, and our heads were laying on a saddle with a blanket thrown over us. There was a lot of contemplation about that in 1960.

Anyway, when Michael Burns did a guest starring on another show, I would go with him. He got a call to go on *Bonanza*, so I went with him and doubled him on that show. I, at the time, looked a lot like Michael Landon and was asked to double him too. Of course, I said yes. I did double him, and he liked me and was asked by Michael Landon if I would stay on *Bonanza* and keep being his double.

I told Michael I was honored for the offer, but I had a great job on *Wagon Train* doubling Michael Burns, and I could not leave him. Michael Landon said he understood and appreciated my loyalty. He then asked if I knew anyone like me who could do the double stunt. I told him I did and would have that person call him and again told Michael how much I enjoyed and appreciated working on the show. I later got a call from my cowboy friend I had referred, thanking me for the reference. He said he got the job and told me that the very first day he worked with him, he shook his hand and handed him a set of car keys. He bought him a new pickup truck, so he wanted to thank me. I knew Michael Landon was a wonderful man, and I was happy for him. That could have been me with a new pickup truck.

Well, that's show business.

Wagon Train Short Stories

Behind the Scenes

On the TV series *Wagon Train*, I was a photo double for the actor Michael Burns, doing his stunts. So we usually shot the *Wagon Train* scenes in Thousand Oaks at the Spahn Ranch. In this particular scene was a buckboard with a man and wife driving a runaway wagon. Wouldn't you just know it, I was dressed as a double for a woman. This, of course, was before there were stuntwomen. The cowboys had a field day teasing me. Thank God the job was over.

Another day on *Wagon Train*, five cowboys were dressed up as Indians. We were to come riding down this big hill, shooting bows and arrows as we were riding. Well, this business was hurry up and wait. So we got to the top of the hill and waited to hear action. We waited and waited. One of the cowboys, I mean Indians, was chewing tobacco. He asked me if I wanted some, and I said, "Why not?" I started chewing, not bad as I was doing as they were, chewing and spitting. Then wouldn't you just know it, they finally called action. All the horses lunged as we took off. My horse lunged so much I swallowed my chew. As we were going down the hill, I got so sick and dizzy. I had a hell of a fall off the horse and rolled down the hill.

As usual on a Western, somebody usually fell off some time. "Rider down!" they called.

"Who? Rene? But he was supposed to be a good rider. Medic, look him over and get him back up the hill. We have to get this shot before it gets dark. Rene, are you okay?

"Yes," I said, "I just lost my grip on the horse." The other cowboys laughed. They never told what happened. We got the shot riding down the hill shooting bows and arrows; all was good.

Rene Veluzat and Michael Burns

Rene Veluzat in double cloth doubling Michael Burns

Hard Ground (2003)

Starring Burt Reynolds
Behind the Scenes

I signed up for a Western movie starring Burt Reynolds and Bruce Dern to come to my movie ranch and film.

I knew my friend Burt Reynolds was in it, and I had not seen him in years, so I was looking forward to seeing him again. So I made special preparations for him. He liked to fly in to the set in a helicopter, so I arranged for that. I conned off a heliport landing zone for him.

First day he landed, and we were all there to greet him. He saw me and came over for a hug. He said, "I may have known. Thanks for setting this up for me." We talked later, and he drove off in a limo to his dressing room to get ready for work.

In the meantime, I got a call on the set to see the director, so I rushed over. My old friend Frank Dobbs, the director from way back, said to me, "Rene, Burt wants you to play the part of the barbwire salesman on the stagecoach."

"Wow! Great, I am thrilled. What do I do?" Just like old times, the stagecoach would get robbed and I would get killed. I could do that. So the stagecoach got robbed, and the actor Martin Kove killed me.

Finally, Burt and I got time to sit in his star wagon dressing room and just talk about good old times we had on all the shows. I thanked him for the part on the show. I really liked Burt Reynolds, what a good friend to have.

Years later, one of the girl passengers who was on the stagecoach came to my movie ranch Blue Cloud as a producer on the show being filmed there. She said she had a present for me. She gave me a picture of me on the stagecoach as the barbwire salesman before I was killed. Wow!

Years after that, on a show in my cave set, a young man who was a camera director said to me, "Rene, my dad said to say hello to you." I asked him who his dad was, and he replied, "Burt Reynolds." Wow, I was blown away. I told him to be sure to tell his dad I said hello too and asked how his mom, Lonnie Anderson, was. He told me she was fine, and he would tell her hello for me too!

Well, you never know who you will meet next! That's show business.

Martin Kove and Rene Veluzat

The Virginian

Starring James Drury
Behind the Scenes

I worked on this show quite a bit as a Virginian ranch hand. I always was doing a lot of horse-back riding. All the actors were great to work with. As usual, in those early days, you would never ask for a picture or an autograph.

Twenty years later, I was with a friend at a fair in Ventura, California, and I saw a sign on one of the buildings that James Drury, star of the TV series *The Virginian*, would be signing autographs.

I said to my friend, "I know him, and I want an autograph."

He said to me, "No, you don't know him."

"Yes, I do."

We rushed over to the building he was in, and there he was, in his Western clothes, with a huge crow around the table where he was signing autographs.

I made my way to the front of the crowd and said to him, "Hi, do you remember me?"

He stood up and said, "Yes, I do." I was amazed, and so was my friend. He said, "You were one of my ranch hands on the show, but forgive me, I do not remember your name."

I said, "Rene."

And he said, "Oh my god, yes." The crowd was getting really excited as two actors from *The Virginian* were there.

I told James, "I loved working with you on the show, but I had only one regret while working on our show." You could hear everyone gasp, including James Drury.

"What, what is your regret, Rene?"

"I am sorry that I did not get a picture or an autograph from you."

James Drury said, "You don't have to worry anymore." He whipped out a picture and auto-graphed it for me, gave me a man hug, and thanked me for being on his show.

"Thank you very much, James." The crowd applauded.

I have that picture hanging on the wall in my office today. I could not believe after all the years that had passed, he still remembered me. That meant a lot to me.

Ironically, as I am writing this chapter about James Drury and my friendship with him, I just learned that he has passed away today, April 6, 2020. It is with great sadness that our actors from the old times are passing away. It has been known that in the entertainment business and movies that actors always pass in pairs of three. Who will be next?

On *The Virginian*, I was honored to be chosen as one of ten cowboys to stage a saloon fight for an important guest. Well, saloon fighting was one of my specialties. "Who is the VIP guest?" I asked. I was told it was a secret until it happened. Well, I thought that was really weird or it was truly a very important VIP guest.

The assistant director said, "Boys, follow me."

We went into a dressing room where we stripped down, and four CIA bodyguards in black suits padded us down looking for what, a hidden gun maybe? I didn't know at the time. They finally gave us cowboys the okay and told us to put our cowboy clothes back on. Then they gave each of us a rubber gun for our holsters. We went back to the saloon and waited about ten minutes. Then all my questions were answered. In walked four more CIA bodyguards with the guest. Oh my god! It was the president of the United States Richard Nixon's wife, Pat Nixon. She wanted to see a saloon brawl. Well, after we were all blown away, we gave a show all right. We all started fighting—threw a fake punch, got thrown into tables and chairs, broke whiskey bottles on one another. I could see she was really enjoying this fight. After about ten minutes later, when everything was broken and we were all lying on the floor, she stood up and said "Bravo!" as she was clapping. Then everyone clapped too.

First Lady Pat Nixon shook our hands personally and thanked each one of us. What an honor to have been chosen to perform for the First Lady of the USA. All the cowboys got a bonus for this, but I bet it cost the studio a lot of money for all the props we broke.

Well, that's show business.

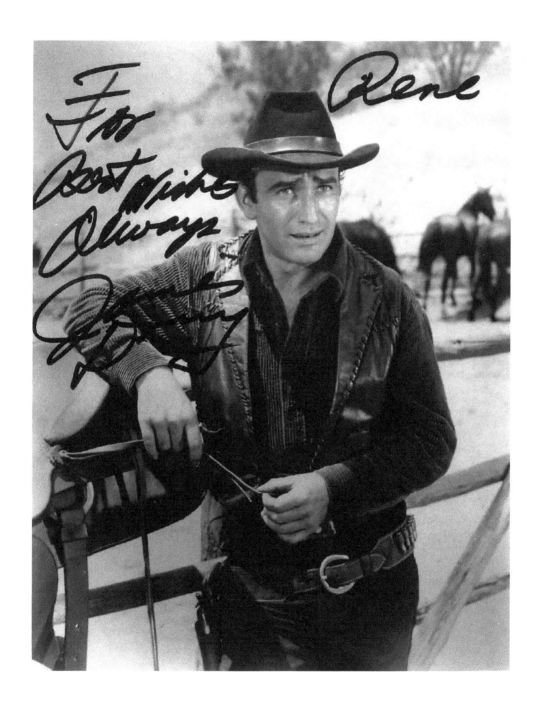

Rene—
Great workin'
with you
on the
Old Virginian
Series!
Randy Boone

CHAPTER 11

Sneaking in the Sets

Knots Landing

Behind the Scenes

WELL, BEING IN the movie business is magical and electrifying. People want to see the stars and how the movies are made. Somehow, the public knows when you are filming with big stars.

It was a TV series entitled *Knots Landing*, and one of the stars at the ranch was Nicollette Sheridan. Yes, I was doing scenes as the Mexican bus driver again while she was going to Mexico in the scene. I had a nice time working with her. She was great!

Incident number 1 happened after the scene on the bus I did with her was done. We thanked each other. Great job. As I was walking from the set, I noticed, on the very top of this big hill, a flash of light. That should not have happened. So I charged up the hill to find a paparazzi cameraman taking pictures with a camera with a two-foot-long zoom lens. I told him he was on my property and was trespassing and to leave, or I would call the cops. He offered me ten thousand dollars to just let him get a shot of the beautiful Nicollette Sheridan. I said *no* and that I would call the cops. He cursed me but finally left.

Incident number 2 was on that same show. There was this young man dressed as a crew member. I noticed him as he just looked different. He had on the same type of clothes, with gloves hanging out of his back pocket and a radio on his belt. We all had this look. I saw him in line for breakfast, lunch, and dinner for three days. But I never saw him during the day. I asked around the other crew members to see if they knew who he was. No one seemed to know him.

So I thought to myself, *This is a clever guy and sneaky too. What could he be up to?* I knew I had to catch this guy, so I waited for lunch with two big guards. Then he came and got in line for a nice studio lunch. I instructed the two guards to go and tell him the owner of the movie ranch wanted to talk to him. He knew then that he was caught. The two guards escorted him discreetly to my office so as not to alarm the production company.

I asked him, "Young man, what the hell are you doing trespassing on my movie ranch? Give me your camera. You are going to jail." As I looked at the film he shot, I was really shocked. He had photographs of all the actors, sets, crew, and production staff and shots of how we were making the movie. "This is terrible!" After I questioned him more, I was screaming at him, "If I told the actors what you have been doing, they would break your neck!"

Some of the pictures looked like he had been on my roof taking pictures. He might have fallen off the roof. I worry about safety a lot. So after scaring the crap out of him, I instructed the guards to take his film, escort him to the street, give him back his camera, and throw him out of the car. I told him that I had his picture, and if he ever showed up at my movie ranch again, he would go to jail. He said he was sorry in a shaky voice and promised to never do it again. He asked me how I knew he was not one of the real crew.

I told him, "Number 1, you were not dusty enough, and number 2, your radio gave you away. We do not use RadioShack radios."

I was glad I caught this guy. He would have sold those pictures for a lot of money.

Barn Set

Behind the Scenes

Past my 50's Town, you would enter the Western sets. I was doing a commercial about a horse being shod around a campfire. Now you never know who is who that would be in the crew. I had always been good about profiling people and what they do. This time, we were all getting ready to film. I looked around and saw the crew. I always checked to see if anybody sneaked onto the set to take pictures. I saw this one guy who looked out of place on the set. So I carefully looked him over as he was wearing a suit, but not a tie.

I eased myself over to him and said, "Hi, are you FBI or CIA?"

The guy immediately froze up and said, "How did you know?"

I told him the better question was what he was doing on my movie ranch. He replied he was with a friend of the special effect guy making the fire. "Well, okay." Then he asked me how I knew he was CIA. I replied, "Well, first thing, you do not look like a crew member, and your mustache is manicured perfectly. And the bulge in your side is probably a nine-millimeter pistol."

He said, "Man, you are good."

I said, "Well, that is one of my jobs, to protect the crew and actors. What brings you to Newhall, California?" He advised he was here on assignment to protect President Clinton when he arrived next week. "Wow, that is great!" We got to talking and became good friends. Some of the things he told me were secrets. We exchanged cards. His was better than mine. He had CIA and stars on his.

CHAPTER 12

Unbelievable Music Videos

The Long Shoot

Behind the Scenes

I LOVE DOING music videos as they are so different. They always have great talent and sometimes big stars. They almost always have very small crews. The downside is, they have hardly any money in their budget to make these videos. I am very good in judging to tell if they are pulling a fast one on me by bringing in huge stars and crews or if they are just trying to do a music video with an unknown talent. I always give them the benefit of the doubt and hope these talents make it.

This one music video put me to the test—fifteen people and the band. They were wonderful people, happy to be filming on a famous movie ranch (Blue Cloud Movie Ranch). They started filming at 6:00 a.m. When 6:00 p.m. came around, the producer said he needed a little more time to finish and said he would pay an additional six hours. I said okay and took the money.

Well, at twelve midnight, the producer came over to me and said he needed more time. They had already now filmed for eighteen hours and needed more time.

"How much more," I asked.

He said, "Just a couple more hours. Here is all the money I have left in my budget."

"Okay, just a couple more hours, and that is it!"

He was excited as he was getting good film of his talent.

This video was really testing me. On the other hand, I felt sorry for them. I wanted them to get all they needed. They all came over and thanked me.

Three hours later, he came over, and I said, "Oh no, you are not done yet? You have been filming for twenty-one hours."

He said, "No, we are not done."

I said, "I cannot let you continue to film anymore. It is not safe."

He said, "We have been taking turns sleeping and then filming. Oh, please let us finish this video. It would mean so much for us." He was holding a hat out and said, "I took up a collection from the crew. Please, will you let us finish? You can have the hat too. It's new."

Oh my god, he was almost crying. I was so tired too. I said in a very loud and meaningful voice, "This is it. At 6:00 a.m., you are done, and I will be shutting off the lights. Give me the hat and go finish." I counted $10.99 in the hat. I did not ever think the shoot could go on that long. I saw it out for twenty-four hours of filming. As they were leaving, they waved and thanked me. I said, "Good luck and go home,"

Trace, Miley, and Billy Ray Cyrus

Behind the Scenes

It seems like I have had a zillion videos at my ranch over my career. They are all different. You never know what they are going to do or how long they plan to shoot or who may show up.

I signed a contract with Trace Cyrus, who was a member of Metro Station, to do a small video with fifteen people. I had never heard of Trace Cyrus.

Trace was supposed to wrestle a chair in a kiddy pool filled with oatmeal. Seemed simple enough? Yeah, right! I should have known better, but I thought, *What the hell, they are going to just shoot a few hours at night. What could go wrong? My son Marcel can handle this little video.* So I went home.

The next day, I called my site rep, my son, Marcel. "How did it go last night?" I asked.

He said, "Dad, you won't believe what happened last night." I told him to calm down and tell me. "Well," he told me, "Trace Cyrus shows up with his band, and everything is good. Then Billy Ray Cyrus shows up and starts to play with Trace. Then, oh my god, all hell breaks out when Miley Cyrus shows up."

Then I said, "You mean the real Miley Cyrus?"

He said, "Yes, yes, it was really her. With her showing up to support her brother Trace, word must have leaked out as eight hundred people wanted to get into the ranch. Dad, I had to call the cops for crowd control. Including the ten guards coming with Miley, it was a total nightmare. After that came the cleanup. What a mess. Thankfully, the producer hired a cleaning crew with a tractor and a dumpster."

Who would have thought a "little music video" would turn out to be that huge?

Willie Nelson

Behind the Scenes

It was a great day for a filming in my 50's Town Movie Ranch. I had a very small feature movie that day. We rented the town for a low-budget picture with twenty people. Now that is not uncommon as we do a ton of low-budget shows all the time.

My son loved doing the small shows. After seventy years in the business, I was trying to take it easy and just do the paperwork (contracts, insurance, etc.) and let him handle the show. But I always liked to double-check everything. So I drove up to the 50's Town to see my son, Marcel, the manager.

I asked him how everything was going. He told me, "All is great. We have just what they said. There are approximately twenty people here, an Andy Gump toilet, one small cube truck, and twenty cars."

"Just like we were told, this is a very low-budget film."

"Okay, so that is why we rented the ranch so cheap."

As I looked around, I saw under an oak tree this million-dollar motor home bus. It was beautiful. I asked Marcel what that was under the oak tree.

He looked and said, "Damn, that looks like a million-dollar motor home."

"Who the hell is in there? Go find out."

Now Marcel was excited. "Maybe we rented the ranch too cheap, what with the million-dollar motor home here. Maybe there is a megastar there." Marcel came back and told me, "It is Willie Nelson. He says he is happy to be here and doing his TV movie I'm with Willie.

I was flabbergasted. We did rent the ranch too cheap. But I said, "It is okay. I love Willie Nelson. Let him do his show. He is a great person, and I am a cowboy."

So you just never know who is going to show up. I am honored to have all these great actors come to my movie ranch.

Master P and Li'l Romeo

Behind the Scenes

This music video I was doing was very different. They were going to have a helicopter land on an eight-by-eight platform. I built it in between the barn and the farmhouse. They were going to have twenty beautiful models and one elephant. Wow! This was what I thought would be a huge video.

So the scene was all set and ready to go. The helicopter was piloted by a friend of mine, Kevin LaRosa. He was an ace pilot. The helicopter was painted like a Gucci handbag. He flew in and landed perfectly on the eight-by-eight platform I had built.

Master P and Li'l Romeo got out, and the beautiful models swarmed around the helicopter. Master P and Li'l Romeo all started to dance and sing along with the elephant. This went on all day.

So one cute thing happened that I just loved. The director called action. The helicopter blades were turning around, the models were dancing with the music, and the elephant was dancing too and shaking its head and stomping its feet. Master P started to sing, then the director suddenly called, "Cut! Where is Li'l Romeo? Somebody find Li'l Romeo."

"Here he is." Master P yelled out, "Get your ass in here and make your million dollars today!"

I thought that was great.

CHAPTER 13

Game Show

Fear Factor

Behind the Scenes

I GOT A call from the location manager of a stunt-and-dare game show called *Fear Factor*, hosted by Joe Rogan. They asked me if I had anything on my 50's Town Movie Ranch that would be exciting and daring.

I said, "Yes, I have the perfect stunt for you." I described my church and a three-hundred-foot runway and my ramp leading into the back of the church.

They asked me, "Well, what do you do?"

I said, "You take a fast car and drive down the runway as fast as you can, up behind the church, and out the huge front window in front and see how far the contestant can jump the car down the 50's Town street."

They were all for that stunt, but they had just one question. "Will that stunt work?"

"I am so confident. I will guarantee you it will work."

"Okay, we are renting your movie ranch and going for this big stunt."

Now I didn't tell them everything, but I did that same stunt on a show called *National Security*, starring Martin Lawrence, so I knew the stunt would work perfectly.

Fear Factor moved in the ranch and began prepping on a nondescript stunt car. They rigged the car with a roll cage and a special harness hanging from the ceiling of the stunt car. When you sit in the special harness seat, you are suspended midair so your body does not hit the seat when you land on the street.

"Okay, here we go. Where is the first contestant?" Everybody started to look for him. Did he chicken out?

As I was looking for him, I heard this god-awful sound from behind the building. I looked there and found him throwing up. I ask him if he was okay.

He said, "In a minute I will be okay." He finished gagging and throwing up. I asked if he was nervous about the stunt, and he said, "No, I got sick eating worms in a contest on this show. Somebody ate more worms than me, so I did not win that one."

I told him to drive full throttle in this car. "Don't be afraid of the jump. You can win this one." I yelled out, "Found him!" And I got him in the car. "Let's go!"

They put him in the car and strapped him in real good. He started the car. I said, "Full throttle and you will win the fifty thousand dollars." He nodded his head. "Remember, full throttle, fifty thousand dollars." He roared in place. The director called action, and he took off like a bat out of hell.

I told the director, "He is going to jump the farthest and win." He came crashing through the church window and bounced down the street. A great jump! Everybody applauded.

The second contestant did his jump but fell short of winning. The winner came over and gave me a hug; he was so excited and, yes, won the fifty thousand dollars too.

The director and producer came over and thanked me too. "This is going to be one of our best episodes."

I was real happy to hear that. As my friend George Peppard of *The A-Team* always said, "I like it when a plan comes together."

CHAPTER 14

Lady Movie Stars

Ellen DeGeneres

Mr. Wrong (1996)
Behind the Scenes

I WAS ON a show where I was getting married to Ellen DeGeneres in the show. I always liked Ellen. But funny things would happen every time a movie star would come to my movie ranch. I always wanted to meet them, no matter who they were or what they were doing. It was just my thing. I liked to know them better as a real person and not a movie character, not in a movie part.

So I asked to meet Ellen. "No problem," I was told. I couldn't believe this, but the studio must like me. They went and got Ellen out of her dressing room. She was just about to do a scene in a wedding dress. They told her the movie ranch owner wanted to meet her and get a picture with her. Now anyone else would probably tell me to take a hike, but not Ellen. She eagerly came out, and I met her.

We were told to get together for the picture. We both squeezed together. She put her arm around me, and I put my arm around her, then the picture was taken. Someone in the crowd yelled out, "Ellen and Rene, say I do!" We did, and everyone laughed and clapped.

I thanked Ellen very much and appreciated her very generous acceptance of my request. She was so great. I have that picture on my office wall today. Did we really get married? Yes, we did moviewise. That is show business.

Rene Veluzat and Ellen DeGeneres get married

Farrah Fawcett

Charlie's Angels (1976)
Behind the Scenes

I was always inspired by Farrah Fawcett's work on *Charlie's Angels*. She was gorgeous and simply nice to people, as I always heard. Now came my chance to find out as she was coming to my movie ranch to film a scene at my cabin in the woods.

As usual, the day came, and she was whisked into her dressing room to get ready for the long day at work. As usual, I asked if I could meet her. Her assistant said, "Of course, Rene, when the appropriate time comes." I waited patiently because they were involved in their character, remembering her dialogue for the scene. After one scene, walking back to her dressing room, it was time. I was there and ready to meet Farrah.

I was introduced to her, and she shook my hand. We talked as we walked on the way back to her dressing room. We talked about the movie ranch, and I told her I loved her in the *Charlie's Angels* series. Then I told her I had worked with Ryan O'Neil on a Nanette Fabray show in 1961. Farrah was really impressed that I had worked with Ryan O'Neil. As we got to her dressing room, I asked her if I could get an autographed picture of her. She said, "Absolutely, yes, it was so nice talking with you."

"Thank you, Farrah."

As I walked away, smiling, I told myself, "Yes, yes, I am going to get a picture."

Oh my god, later that day, how things could change in a minute. Over the walkie-talkie, I heard Farrah had tripped over the camera dolly track and knocked herself out. Oh my god, everybody was worried and upset as the ambulance took her to the hospital. Filming was halted, and they wrapped and left. I was so worried I called the hospital and her assistant and was told she would be okay. Thank God, what an experience.

I forgot all about the picture I wanted to get from Farrah. I figured, well, that was not going to happen. One month later, I was delivered a large envelope with her picture autographed to me. I could not believe it! She really is a great person.

Jenny McCarthy

1994 Playmate of the Year
Behind the Scenes

Jenny McCarthy came to my deserted Mexican town to film. I will never forget her driving up in her white Jeep to film her Playmate video.

I introduced myself to her and offered to assist her if she needed anything during the day of filming. There were a few things she needed during the day; no big deal. But she thought that I had helped her and that it was huge. She did a great job on her *Playboy* video. I knew she would be huge in the business.

She was so nice and autographed her script to me. To me that was huge. I will forever cherish the fact that Jenny was so nice and easy to work with. I am so happy for her success.

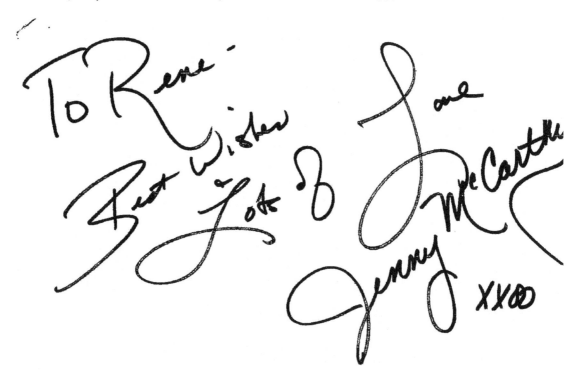

Michael Trikilis Productions
1994 Playmate of the Year
Jennifer McCarthy
February 28–March 2, 1994

Rene Veluzat and Jenny McCarthy

Anna Nicole Smith

Skyscraper (1996)
Behind the Scenes

I got a call to do a scene with a girl at my barn on a Sunday. I said, "I do not want to do it. It is Sunday." I worked six long days this week. A studio day is almost always sixteen hours for the driver's crew. We never see our homes in the daylight.

As he was trying to convince me, I finally said, "Okay, who is the actress?"

He said, "Anna Nicole Smith."

Then I said, "Okay, we are going to do this. Only one condition is, I get to meet Anna Nicole Smith."

"Okay, no problem. Anything else?"

"Just location fees," I said as I laughed.

"No problem, Rene."

Sunday came, and we were all waiting for Anna. Then she came. Just like all the other *Playboy* models, she was beautiful. I thought to myself, *I am so lucky to have all these* Playboy *models and actresses come to my movie ranch, and I get to meet them firsthand.*

Anna was told, "The ranch owner wants to meet you."

"Okay, let's do it," was her reply. As we were walking over to meet, I was trying to hide my excitement and just be me.

"Hi, Anna. I'm Rene, and I am so happy to meet you."

She shook my hand, gave me a hug, and whispered in my ear, "I like you."

As chills ran down my spine, I said in her ear, "I like you too." Then they took a great picture of us. We hugged goodbye, and she went to work. As she walked away, I said thank you, and she smiled at me.

Now you and I both know this is Hollywood movie talk. One can dream, but it was fun. I really liked Anna and followed her career up and down until her death on February 8, 2007. I was deeply saddened, as was many millions of other people were. But I felt special as I had gotten to talk, laugh, and hang out with her that Sunday. That was great, really great.

Through the years, I often thought of her when one of her movies or pictures would trigger a thought of her and that brief meeting on that Sunday. She was just special, and that stuck to me. This might sound crazy, but I always wanted to visit her grave thinking that would give me closure. But she was buried in the Bahamas. Who goes there?

Well, the opportunity came up to take a vacation to the Bahamas with some of our friends. The vacation was arranged, and off I flew to the Bahamas. I held off telling everyone I would like to visit Anna's grave site. Wasn't too sure how my friends would take that as they had never met her. So when I told them of my wish, they all got quiet and said, "Go ahead if you want, but you are crazy." Okay, so I was crazy, but I wanted to do it.

We were now in the Bahamas on a tour, having a wonderful time. I told myself it was now or never. "Who wants to go with me and see Anna Nicole Smith's grave site?"

It got quiet, then one of my good friends, Tarlena, said, "Okay, Rene, I will go with you."

So my wife Patti, Tarlena, and I got a taxi and told the taxi driver to take us to Lake View Memorial Gardens. He freaked out and said he could not take us there.

"Why?"

"That is where Anna Nicole Smith is buried, and it is heavily guarded." He said he could not drive us there.

I thought two things: (1) that it was good that she was buried there and we were on the right track and (2) it was bad she was guarded. I had to think of something quick; we came all this way, and we were in a taxi one mile from the cemetery.

Okay, so I pulled out a fifty-dollar bill. His eyes lit up, and he said, "Okay, I will drive you around the cemetery." That worked for me.

We were driving around the cemetery, and I told him to pull over and give me five minutes. He put his hand out, and I handed him another fifty dollars. He pulled over, and Tarlena and I jumped out of the taxi with my trusty Nikon camera ready to go. Patti waited in the taxi, probably scared to death, thinking we were all going to end up in the Bahamas jail just because of me. "You are crazy, Rene, just for a picture of Anna's grave site."

Tarlena and I were frantically looking for a gate to get into the cemetery. All of a sudden, a guard jumped out of nowhere. "HALT! HALT! What are you doing here?"

"We are looking for the gate to get in to visit a friend."

He said, "You cannot go in there." I reached in my pocket and pulled another fifty dollars. He took it and told us we had five minutes.

We found the gate, climbed over the fence, and scrambled to get over a five-foot bush fence. The guard pointed out the headstone and then disappeared. We finally were over the fence looking for Anna's grave, and we finally found it. We raced toward it. It was beautiful, just like I thought it would be. It was five feet tall and about ten feet wide, dark brown with platinum scrolling on the headstone. I took a picture of Tarlena by the headstone, and she took one of me. Tarlena and I scrambled to get out of the cemetery. As we were running to climb over the fence, I said goodbye to Anna and said a little prayer at the grave site.

Now I was hoping our taxi was still there with my wife, Patti. Yeah, they were still there. We jumped into the taxi and asked to be taken back to our ship. As we said goodbye to the taxi driver, I gave him a fifty-dollar tip and thanked him. To me I just had closure, and it was a relief to have had the opportunity to do this. What an experience!

Anna Nicole Smith and Rene Veluzat

Rene at the grave site of Anna Nicole Smith

Lake View Memorial Gardens

Tia Carrere

Behind the Scenes

This is a cute story about a supergorgeous model, Tia Carrere, who came to my movie ranch to do a photo shoot. They arrived with a small crew of about ten people to do the photo shoot. So naturally, as the owner of the movie ranch, I was going to be there to see that everything was going to go well for the superstar model. It has always been my number 1 priority to ensure the safety of the people who come to my movie ranch to film, no matter who they are. I always watch out for them wherever they go and whatever they do, to see that everything is safe.

The first thing was, the wardrobe man forgot the changing bag for Tia to change her wardrobe in. They called me over to help hold a makeshift bag of packing blankets to hold in a circle for Tia to change in. The wardrobe guy said jokingly, "Rene, don't look." We all laughed, and Tia said, "If Rene has not seen it, now is the time." Well, we all laughed.

So this went on all day. I really enjoyed this day, as you can imagine, and Tia and I became "good friends." I got her a lot of props to use in the photo shoot—baskets, netting, old chairs, and old miscellaneous props.

So it was called out, "This is the last shot of the day. Tia, take your position for this set of shots."

She walked in, dressed in a black negligee, and she said, "I want Rene and me to do this shot." I could have fallen over. She wanted me in her photo shoot. "Rene, get in here," Tia said. I did get in there with Tia, and we did the photo shoot. I thanked her and the crew.

As she was leaving, Tia said, "Thank you for all your help. See you in the magazine."

These are some of the unexpected things that happened to me. Lucky Pierre! That's me.

Tia Carrere

Tia Carrere

MY HIGH ADVENTURES BEHIND THE MOVIE SCENES

Ann Jeffreys

Topper TV Series
Behind the Scenes

My accidental meeting with Ann Jeffreys was when I went to a Golden Boot Award function. Now the Golden Boot Awards is for cowboy actors to receive their awards. This is an awards show along the same theme as the Academy Awards for all the other actors. This one is just for cowboys. I was invited as I played many cowboys over the years. I was invited to go to this event with my cowboy friends and models who modeled for Frederick's of Hollywood.

My wife Patti and I were picked up in a limo, and we were all dressed up in our cowboys' finest. As we arrived at the Hollywood Hotel, our limo pulled up at the red carpet, and we got out. Fans were yelling, clapping, and taking pictures of us. Boy, that was great. Maybe some of them actually recognized me. What a thrill! I was really enjoying this as I waved back to them.

We all walked down this long red carpet into this huge hotel room where they had tables of memorabilia. This was all part of a silent auction for charity. What do you do? You walk around until you find something you like, then you put your name on the list along with your bid amount.

Okay, so I walked around looking at all the really neat stuff. I saw a Roy Rogers gun and holster set he used in the movies. I really wanted the set as he was one of my all-time favorite cowboys. So I wrote my name on the bid sheet. Next to the Roy Rogers set was the John Wayne set. I could bid on it if I did not get Roy's set. I walked around and came back to see if anyone had outbidden me, and sure enough, someone had. So I upped my bid and walked around again. When I came back, someone had outbidden me again, and the price was getting up there. I was frustrated. Then I felt a tap on my shoulder, and this beautiful lady said to me, "Young man, I see you are bidding on both sets of guns. Which one do you really want?" To my surprise, it was Ann Jeffreys, star of one of my favorite TV series *Topper*. What a surprise! I was so close to her. She said, "Let's make a deal. I won't bid on Roy Rogers's, and you quit bidding on John Wayne's [the one she really wanted]." I guess we were bidding against each other on both sets. When the bidding was over, I got the Roy Rogers set, and she got the John Wayne set for a friend of hers.

I could not begin to tell you how excited I was to get the set I wanted and to be standing next to Ann Jeffreys. I asked if I could get a picture with us together. She was in a beautiful royal-blue Western dress, and she squeezed up to me in my black gamblers outfit. I have the picture hanging in my office today. I will always cherish that moment. Ann is one of the most gracious, elite, and beautiful women I have ever met. Then we both said thank you and went into the awards ceremony.

It was about one week later that our local newspaper hunted me down to do a story about my movie experiences and about the purchase of the Roy Rogers 1938 limited edition gun set authorized by Roy Rogers from the early year's series. At the time, I did not realize how important and valuable the set was. The local newspaper *The Signal* put me and the famous gun set on the front page!

This is really funny as I am reading the article about me in August 1997. I talked about my life in the movies and about writing a host of colorful stories from my past and the hope to have them published in the near future. Well, that future is now, twenty-three years later. Boy, do I have a lot of stories to tell now.

Ann Jeffreys and Rene Veluzat

Patti and Rene going to the Telly Awards show

Rene and Patti Veluzat at the awards show

CHAPTER 15

About the Author

I KNOW A story of Hollywood, and Hollywood knows one of me. I have had a life in the bright shadows of pictures. In this drama of dramas, I am unofficially a witness, a participant, a storyteller of parts.

Somewhere there is the image of me as a surly youth. I am blustering before a half-hesitating, half-whispering Ronald Reagan in a General Electric Theater production. This image is turning into magenta, the color of deterioration, the color of film stock disintegrating into dust.

Tomorrow I will still be here. A picture car driver, a condor operator, or a set decorator will drive along the five miles of dirt road to the Rene Veluzat Motion Picture Ranch and remember me from other projects. They wonder if I will be there strolling between the standing sets, the modern-day town, the dilapidated gas station, the remains of the Western buildings, still ready to advise on explosions, still able to provide the framework for silver screen destruction.

I started my career in a more benevolent era, one where the Children's Motion Picture Guild, out of its largess, thought a waterskiing lesson across a high alpine lake was necessary for advancement. I spent my teen years with Ricky Nelson, goofing around a television malt shop.

I have had my embraces with deep-waisted Playmate centerfolds memorized by the camera's uncritical eye. Tony Curtis and Lorenzo Llamas had gripped me in manly hugs. Ellen DeGeneres posed as my wife.

My body was crosshatched with scars from stunt falls and the ingress and egress of an errant bullet. My face was frequently used in the background to add color.

I could trace my European antecedents back to Champlain, France. The name Veluzat is still a local one, and I could pass with beret and crusty bread as one of the populace. (I've tried this.) I have the peasant's pervasive love for lore and magic and the belief in the necessity of myths. So it was not so unusual for me to have taken to picture making. Even painting fences when I was five led to this. Working in movies was as natural to me as any trade that required a wrench or plow.

I could start my stories anywhere. A restaurant in Canyon Country would remind me of Yvonne De Carlo eating charmingly in its back booth. Names of faded glory, mentioned in passing, would bring back impressions of their most vivid days. But I would begin like a tarot reading, my hands passing over the cards until I was warned by the one with the most heat, my mind still impressed by the brightness.

I was aware of a symmetry in my life that began when I was still little. Whatever I needed would come to me. Whatever I feared would find me. I saw patterns emerging that I never designed, reoccurring cantos on the themes of my far too human frailties. Sometimes it took years for the last act to unfold, but when it did, it was always appropriate. I had known poetic justice in startling ways. I answered the phone, and it was the voice of an unrequited love from twenty years past. After a night of restless nightmares, I arrived on the set to meet someone who answered my most desperate dreams. Nothing had ever come easy to me, but having been hard-won, I was usually too wrung out afterward to enjoy my triumphant deed. It had led me to believe in the psychic telling, for whatever was predicted for me would invariably arrive.

There were ways to cover the signs of poverty. Poverty is not merely a station in life, it is a division between shame and pride. We knew how to pretend we were not poor. I knew this complicity from the very start. No other child of five I knew worked with his father painting walls on the side of the road. I was digging trenches under houses and helping my father lower them. I went to work with him building and relocating houses. I did the labor of an adult, and it was expected of me never to protest. The money I brought in barely disguised our circumstances, but it was enough that we made the effort to look like everyone else.

Until I was late in my teens, I never knew the feel of new clothes. I feared comment on this. If I was asked where I got my clothes, I used references to the most elitist stores. We lived in Huntington Park during the week and the ranch in Saugus on the weekends, but I told everyone that we shopped for our clothes in Beverly Hills.

My mother devised our wardrobes, picking through the racks of the Salvation Army for what could be refurbished as new with needle and thread. She washed our shirts and pants of every stain, ironed them crisply, and put in creases that would gladden an inspecting officer. We were bidden never to tell how we managed on our paltry income. It was part of our family honor to appear normal. We were able to maintain this attitude even though the car we drove around town was a very, very old one, with the muffler dragging low.

It is now hilarious to me the ruses we pulled. In the new age of television, we were the last of our acquaintances to acquire a set. It was very small with only a ten-inch screen. We watched Beany and Cecil and Sheriff John through a blizzard of snow and fuzzy lines. Still, we were thrilled ceaselessly to own such a devise. For years, we subsisted on only an antenna on the roof. Just an antenna, no television. Once again, to appear to go without would signal our deficient means. We had observed how others who failed economically were taunted and bullied. We lived in the penumbra of humiliation and fear. We would sacrifice the truth rather than be the object of scornful jeers. It was understood we would never receive such ignominies. I believe I was the one who suggested we plant the useless antenna.

When I was ten, my mother got the brain scheme to enter me in the Boy Next Door contest. She had exalted hopes that I would attain fame in the entertainment world. This was one of the steps she took. It was in a mild way a beauty contest, because the recipient of the award would secure a modeling assignment with Desmond's Clothes, a large clothing chain in Los Angeles. Other than having the lavish love of my mother, I never thought I was any more or less ideal than any other kid on the block. Maybe it was my smile. Even through my family's adversities, I always had a ready smile. Maybe that was what won me the title. Certainly no one could have foreseen it. Only when it happened was it verified that I was someone special.

For the first time, I wore new clothes. They looked so beautiful, fresh from the factory, the colors rich and pure. I could barely believe I would be the first to wear them. My body welcomed their taunt seams and tight button holes. They did not have that odd staleness that accompanied secondhand clothes or that flaccid quality, the result of numerous hot water washings.

I modeled in shows at the Biltmore Hotel, in the Blossom Room, other hotels, other stages in parks, and meeting facilities. My job was to walk from one end of the stage or platform to the other. The audience's attention fed me; I loved showing off. I wore Desmond's suits, their clothes, their ties, pretending they were really mine. But at the end of the day, I had to give back the new, fashionable clothes. All that I really obtained was a plaque. It still hangs on my wall.

It was from my insecurities that my personality formed. It was something very deep inside me, in my mind and soul, that clothes mattered, that if I worked hard enough, I could have new clothes. I always wanted new clothes, not the castoffs I was forced to wear. It was beyond wanting to look in vogue, though I did covet wingtip shoes and sports jackets. Ah yes, sports jackets. It was about acceptance and being thought good enough, projecting the right look. It sounded shallow to say I looked to clothes to define me, but in a business made up of visual clues, clothes had to be stylish, or else you were passed over.

And then there were the compliments from girls. My first new pair of pants were a pair of white corduroy Levi's with a tiny cuff at the bottom and pleats in the front. I could still remember the pride I felt in wearing those new pants. Rene, the girl I was dating in high school, complimented me on those pants. The elation I felt at being noticed like that struck me very deeply. Sexual thrills and the thrill of new clothes became intimately entwined. To this day, I have a very large wardrobe. Each outfit I purchased hearkened back to that basic stimuli. When I dressed, even if it was only to don a down vest, plaid wool shirt, and jeans to grade a road with only the neighbors' swayback horses to admire me, I made sure my attire was meticulous.

Looking one's sartorial best seemed to have been a common acclimation for other poor boys as well. I was on a movie set with George Hamilton when he told a story similar to mine. George, who looks to be the manor born or, rather, the resort born, is a man who wears collars and cuffs with the aplomb of an ambassador. His parents were not rich, but they had high aspirations for him. His mother's rationale was if he looked good and he believed he was good, it would follow; he would get the part. George not only looked good but he also made the part indelibly his. From that first secondhand tuxedo, purchased from the charity bin, came a life of playboy roles and jet set escapades. My mother also refitted a used tuxedo for me, and I, too, have often enjoyed the warm surge of fine wine and a mellow cigar in my parallel Dickensonian tale.

The nicest clothes I ever wore for a role were the ones identical to Robert Wagner's, in the television series *It Takes a Thief*. Frequently it was my hand, in the hand inserts, seen writing a letter or focused on while turning a key in a lock. They used me to double him walking away, driving his car, or creeping along a wall. They cut those suits from the most sumptuous cloth—cool silk, fine spun wool, cotton as soft as kid skins. The camera's discerning eye demanded special attention to unseen linings, meticulously cut shirts that never emerged beneath precision-stitched jackets, hems that hung with the perfect allowances. In the vestments of a debonair jewel thief, I assumed the character's calm, cool demeanor. I could pantomime turning the combination on a safe as I once did, my slow, steady movements influenced by the elegance of that attire. For me, acting starts from the outside and textures the man within.

Clothes were not the only things restored to look like new in my boyhood. Toys, too, came from that generous organization, the Salvation Army. We were overjoyed to receive new toys at Christmas and assumed they were just made. It was hardly the case in our meager circumstances. But we never knew it, like we never knew the true identity of Santa Claus. My parents did what they could to create joy in the season, when in reality, our sparse straits had not changed. The night before Christmas, my father would straighten out what was bent, spruce up the dull to make it shiny—in short, return the toys to their former luster. But in the morning, we always wondered why our hands would be red from riding our bicycles. We assumed that Santa Claus had entered our order at the last minute and there was not enough time for the elves at the assembly plant to properly dry our little trucks and cars.

My first car was a wreck. It had never even been driven before. It had fallen off the car carrier before it could receive ownership. The only way we could afford a car for me was to purchase the remains of a car that had been totaled. My father, aided by a body guide, taught me how to put the car together. My bedroom was the laboratory for this reincarnation. All the salvageable parts lay strewn on the floor. By increments, we bought equivalents to take the place of the mangled remains. Working together, we restored my 1957 Mercury Monterey as it should have been. Owning a set of hot wheels like this increased my status phenomenally in high school. It served to foreordain the standard I so desired to secure.

My two younger brothers and I always loved mechanical toys. From our earliest days, we were always taking apart and reconstructing all kinds of transports. Those rejuvenated toys eventually made way to all manner of real operating trucks, cars, buses, and even jeeps.

Part of my father's many ways of turning a buck was dealing in Army surplus. This was how I got started in one of my larger ventures. I began by acquiring military earners with an ambitious measure. Then I used my stock to furnish the pictures with prop vehicles. From my considerable cache, I gained versatile experience. I could drive anything. In fact, for the movies, I have accomplished driving them all, mostly in scenes of peril.

I drove the police tank in *Dragnet* for Dan Aykroyd and Tom Hanks. This was actually an Army reconnaissance tank, which was painted the color of the LA police uniform, a dark blue. Most evident was an impressively long battering ram protruding like an elongated penile projectile. Attached to the shaft of the ram was a metal placard with a police shield emblazoned and the proclamation "Have a nice day." The tank had been in storage for a while and needed to be thoroughly checked out and properly sealed, which I attended to myself.

I have been blessed with so many good things in life. I have had my ups and downs, but so many good things have happened to me. Being married to my wife, Patti, and having a son, Marcel, were the best things that ever happened. I owned three very successful movie ranches, had been Man of the Year in 1975, had a very successful real estate business, was a general contractor, owned a protection company (Titanium Protection), was a teamster in Local 399, was a studio driver, and so many other things. I am fortunate to do what I want to do, go wherever I want, and buy whatever I want. I am very happy.

Some of my downsides were when I was ten years old, at the racetrack, a horse kicked me and broke my leg, then I got the measles while I had a cast on my leg. I was scratching my leg with a coat hanger. Then years later, at the racetrack, when my Dad and I raced our horses, our groom, who takes care of our horses, found a big snake around the horse feed. He picked it up and started to swing it around. I was in the crowd watching. He wound it up, and the snake slipped out of his hand and was coming through the air right toward me. The snake landed on my neck. The head went one way, and the tail the other way around my neck. The snake was mad, and it bit me on the chest. I passed out! The next thing I remember was, I was looking at the clouds. My vision was very blurry, and I was dizzy. I thought I was on my way to heaven, that I was dead! A few minutes later, a doctor leaned over me and told me I was not going to heaven, that I was in the hospital. I was going to be very sick for a while, but I would live. Well, that was good news.

Well, years later, I came home from work at night in my new Ford F-150 truck, all painted up with scalloped paint job and big tires. All of a sudden, coming down the hill, I blew my front left tire, which threw me out of balance. The truck turned over on its top and was skidding uncontrollably down the hill. As the truck was rotating around and around, after skidding about one thousand feet, I came to rest between a telephone pole and an oak tree. After I figured out I was upside down, I finally got out of the truck, and a nice neighbor let me use their phone to call Patti for help. She came and got me. Well, I was saved again. Lucky Pierre.

My love for flying airplanes and helicopters went way back to a little town called Mettler Station, California, with a population of fifty people. When you drive through the town, you would pass a small gas station and a coffee shop, and you were out of town. I loved going there to see my uncle. He had a nice Cessna airplane I loved to fly. This was a cotton farming area, and I loved to fly the old crop duster airplane too.

So fast-forward to my movie ranch. One of my helicopter buddies flew over, and I signaled him to land. He was flying a switcher three-blade, three-seat Bell 300 helicopter. He landed, and we talked. He said, "Rene, come to my house and fly my new rebuilt Bell 47 helicopter. I just spent a year rebuilding it." I said okay. A couple of days later, I was at his house. There in the field was his beautiful Bell 47 helicopter on the landing pad. So we did the flight check, got in, warmed it up to speed, and took off. We were flying all over Newhall, and I was taking pictures. What a beautiful helicopter, and what a nice flight.

Then my buddy, the helicopter pilot and owner, told me to put my camera down and fly the helicopter. I did, and now I was the pilot in control. So now I was flying his beautiful helicopter, and it was flying so smooth and steady. I told him he did a good job rebuilding the helicopter. After two hours enjoying flying, I suddenly realized I had a show in the 50's Town this afternoon, and I needed to take the helicopter back to the barn. So I flew back to his house and told him to take the controls so he could land. Okay, new pilot in command, so I sat back as he circled the land. All of a sudden, something went wrong. Red light came on the dash as a warning bell sounded; we were dropping out of the sky very fast. The pilot said we were going to crash. So my fear kicked in, and I suddenly realized this was it. I was sure I was going to die this time.

As the helicopter was charging straight down to earth, the pilot was frantically trying to control the helicopter to no avail. My entire life flashed before me in split second, from the time I was born to the present. I told myself I did not want to die, that I had lots of things yet to do. *I love my wife and son. I don't want to die yet, God.* I braced for impact. The pilot's training kicked in just as we were going to hit the ground. He flared the nose up, which brought the tail down, broke the tail off, and now we were going about fifty miles an hour in, of all places, a trailer park. Now we were bouncing off trees and trailers. People were running out of the way as we headed straight for the swimming pool. The broken, mangled helicopter came to rest just before going into the swimming pool. People were terrified, and so was I. Two guys pulled the pilot out, but my door wouldn't open. I was yelling for them to break the door. The fuel tanks was over my head, and any minute, I could explode. The two guys ripped the door off its hinges and pulled me to safety. As the pilot and I were dragged under an oak tree, we looked at the totaled-out helicopter. "What the hell just happened?" The pilot said we had a bad malfunction. You got that right!

As we were lying under the oak tree, we were checking to see if we still had arms, legs, and teeth and all our functions. Any minute, the cops, fire engines, and paramedics would come help us. After about an hour, I said, "I do not think anyone will be coming to check us. After all, this is a very bad helicopter crash." You would have thought someone had called the cops. Maybe we landed in a dope-and-drug trailer park, and they did not want the cops there. I said, "Help me up. I got to work." We helped each other up, dragged myself in pain to my truck, and got to the 50's Town Movie Ranch. I managed to get the gates open and do the movie. As they were filming, I was laid out in my truck, not as worried too much about my pain as to how I was going to explain all this to my wife.

I got home, and of course, I could barely walk. I was beat up, and now everything was swelling up. Both eyes were black, and she said "What the hell happened to you this time?"

"Well, honey, would you believe I went to a cowboy bar with my friends, had a little too much to drink, and fell of the barstool?"

She said, "I would never believe that. What the hell happened?" So I told her. Patti first said I could have been killed.

"Yes, Patti, now I need you to take me to my favorite chiropractor in the morning."

The chiropractor examined me and told me I was two inches shorter. "What happened?"

"Would you believe I fell off a barstool?"

He said, "No, what really happened?" I told him the story, and he said I was lucky to be alive. I asked if he could fix me, and he said, "Yes, but you do not have many fixing left."

"Okay, I will be more careful."

He said, "You stunt guys are keeping me in business."

A couple of days later, I dreaded the call from the FAA (Federal Aviation Administration). He asked if I was flying a helicopter in the last couple of days that crashed in a trailer park.

I said, "Yes, sir, I was flying that helicopter earlier in the day, but I let the pilot, who is the owner of the helicopter, land it."

"Well, what happened?"

"We had a hard landing, but no one got hurt."

"Well, send me a report on that, and that will be it."

"Okay, thank you." Boy, was I relieved. No one got hurt but me. I was lucky God was with me that day. Three months later, I was good to go.

By the way, all these stories I am telling you in this book are true stories, as unbelievable as they are. It could only happen to me.

Well, I semiretired in 2015 when I sold Blue Cloud Movie Ranch. I thought my life would get easier, maybe a little. I still owned a movie ranch, but I turned it over to my son, Marcel, to run. But I still oversee it.

Well, it happened again. God was testing me. In June 2017, I was with the gardener as he was clearing weeds on my ten-acre home property. I told him not to set the hot weed eater down in the weeds. Well, would you just know it. He did and caught the hill on fire. I saw the hill burning up toward the property next to mine, which was a preschool for kids, and it was headed toward the town of Newhall. I was in a panic. I sent the gardener with a garden hose to put out the fire. But it was blazing too high. I called for help as I ran to the preschool next door and told them there was a fire and they should evacuate now.

As I ran back to my property, the fire department, police, and forest department with a fire-fighting helicopter dropping water got the fire out. The school was saved, and the town of Newhall was saved. What a deal that was. When all the excitement was over, I could hardly breathe. I thought it was all the smoke. Well, it got worse the next day and even worse that night. About 10:00 p.m., I fell on the floor, gasping for air. I managed to call my wife, Patti, in the other room to help me up. I told her I could not breathe and maybe I should go to the hospital like she had been telling me. She got me in her car and took me to the emergency room at Henry Mayo Hospital in Newhall. A nice sheriff helped me out of the car and into the hospital. They immediately gave me oxygen. Right away, I felt better.

"Okay, let's go home."

The doctor said, "Hold on. Check him in, and let's do some tests." After the tests, the doctor asked my wife, "How is he able to breathe at all? Every artery is plugged up."

So here was how it ended. I spent sixteen days in the hospital and had a new aortic valve replaced, along with a four-way bypass. That was all it took to fix me again. God was right there with me again. Thank God.

These short stories are true—things that happened, good and bad and funny. I was there for these as a movie ranch owner of three movie ranches. One of my jobs was to show the location managers the locations to see if they would work for them and for their TV show or movie.

After being in the movie business for seventy years, I had seen thousands of producers, stars, location managers, crew, and publicity people. I had built three very successful movie ranches, one being the one-hundred-acre Blue Cloud Movie Ranch. In the year 2000, I decided to go for it or broke. They called me Lucky Pierre (that being my middle name). So I purchased one hundred acres in Santa Clarita, California. It was in an isolated valley in which people had dumped trash for twenty years. I had a dream of this property to become the number 1 movie ranch. The local paper, the *Newhall Signal*, called it the Ranch of Dreams.

As I struggled with my other two movie ranches to make money to clean up Blue Cloud and build sets, I did acting, many stunts, transportation, and renting out props and transportation. I began to buy Army trucks and helicopters, along with other military equipment, such as Army tents, Army boxes, anything Army. As I was cleaning all the trash from Blue Cloud and moving in my Army equipment and tents for the Army camp I was building, I was also doing small shows. I could remember the very first show at Blue Cloud was a soccer ball commercial for France. I dug a foxhole trench one hundred feet long for the show. Just prior to that, there was a large fire in Santa Clarita that burned all the rest of the trash on the property. Lucky Pierre (me).

Some location managers said it was a hundred acres of hills and valleys that were charcoaled— in other words, everything was black and burnt. Maybe, but the location manager for the soccer commercial said it was perfect for their battlefields, and they rented it for their commercial. Then the word got out that Rene, with his new movie ranch on Blue Cloud Road, would be perfect for military shows. Then came my big break—the *JAG* TV series! They were there for almost all their shows, with David James Elliott, Catherine Bell, and the producers of *JAG*. We all became great friends.

Then my other big break was when *JAG* ended. Then came the same producers for *NCIS*. They began filming almost every episode at my ranch. Mark Harmon, the lead actor, and I became good friends. I began building my movie sets as fast as possible. The Army camp had twenty-five Army trucks and Hummers, seven Army Huey helicopters (some wrecked for crash scenes), and fifteen Army tents. It was a pretty intense Army camp for filming.

Then I completed my huge Middle Eastern city, along with my cave. We filmed *Scooby Do! Curse of the Lake Monster*, among other shows, in the cave. I also built a vintage '50s-style gas station. I was buying anything I thought would rent that no one else had. So I bought a Cessna 150 airplane in a little town called Paso Robles in the wine country. So I took my truck and trailer to Paso Robles to the small airport and bought the plane. I had to take it apart to fit on my trailer, but I brought it home to my house, where it sat in pieces for almost two years. After two years, my wife, Patti, said I should move it to the movie ranch. So that was when I built the airplane hangar to put it in. So now I have a small airport with a graded dirt runway for the plane. The airplane hangar was huge, with just a small Cessna airplane in it. So I decided it needed company. Prior to all this, I worked a show called *Dante's Peak*, starring Pierce Brosnan and Linda Hamilton. They had four crashed helicopters I wanted to buy when they were done with the movie. They said they were already sold. Bummer!

I got a lucky break. Someone called me to tell me there was an auction sale in the desert and there would be helicopters for sale. I went there and bought five helicopters, and would you just know it, they were from the show *Dante's Peak*. Ha ha, I got them at last. I purchased one helicopter that was perfect and brought them in the airplane hangar at Blue Cloud Movie Ranch. They started to work immediately. Good deal for me. Blue Cloud became a huge success for me, doing big TV series and feature movies like *Iron Man 1* and *2* and *American Sniper* with Bradley Cooper. And I got to meet and talk with Clint Eastwood, a giant in the business. We had some great talks. He autographed his *American Sniper* script to me. So how much more greatness can you ask for? I have been so blessed. I got everything I ever wanted.

Shortly thereafter, I was doing an Army promo for the government. The scene was for a Hummer to come down the hill and stop. That was the scene.

"Rene, we want to rent your Middle Eastern town and a Hummer."

Okay, I always think of safety. "Okay, who will drive the Hummer?" I was told an Army guy. Okay, at Blue Cloud, for twenty years and all the shows, approximately one hundred per year, with the movies and big shows where three hundred cars and trucks, semis, honey wagons, special effects semis in and out were used, six hundred cars a day for twenty years, there had been no problems. Thank God. And all the helicopters that flew in, no problems. If I did not like the pilot or what he was going to do, they did not do it at Blue Cloud. Well, the day came, and the government show was here.

I said, "Who is going to drive the Hummer?" Five Army guys said they would. "Okay, get in and start the Hummer." The first Army guy got in and looked around. I said, "Start it."

He said, "Where is the key?" I was shocked. All five Army guys could not find the key *because there was no key*! It is a toggle switch on the dash.

So I knew none of these actors were real Army guys and none knew how to drive a Hummer. I asked the director to tell me what the real scene for the Hummer was. He told me what the new scene was, and I was in shock that they had not told me what was to happen. Well, we changed it.

"All right, what do you want the Hummer to do?"

The director told me he wanted the Hummer to come down the hill as fast as it could, with one soldier on the turret firing the .50-caliber machine gun and the second soldier in the back and one in front all firing machine guns while bombs were going off under the Hummer. The Army soldier driver tried to avoid the bombs. But to no avail, the Hummer got blown up, and they all died. I asked if he had a stuntman on set to do this safely. Then the director freaked out.

"All right, I can help you. I am a stuntman, and I have done this for fifty years. I will be your stuntman and drive the Hummer for your shot and give you what you want safely."

The director was now very thankful for me to do this. "Send this man to wardrobe."

"No, thanks," I replied. "I have my own Army outfit. Give me five minutes." I was back in five minutes in my Army outfit.

"Okay, load up, soldier."

They got their guns and blank ammo ready. They gave me my starting mark. Now doing this for fifty years, I was not taking any chances. I made my own end stop marks. I marked my left side on a wall, right side, and also a large rock for the front tire to stop me. One of the marks was going to work. We were ready. I backed up the hill and called ready. Special effects called out they were hot and ready with their bombs and smoke and us firing blanks at them. The director called action.

I took off with my soldiers firing. All hell broke loose as I came down this Middle East road. It was my sole responsibility, with the lives of the soldiers in the Hummer and mine, to be able to finish the stunt. As I approached the end, more intense bombs went off, with a tremendous amount of smoke. I was able to hit my mark and make the shot. As we all got killed in the gunfire and bombs, some soldiers fell out of the Hummer and landed on the ground to die. I shook as the bullets hit me, and I died at the wheel of the Hummer.

As the smoke cleared, I heard the director call, "Cut! Beautiful, wonderful, print it."

I then noticed they had placed a cameraman ten feet directly in front of the Hummer. I realized that if I had missed my mark, I would have run over the cameraman and killed him. Then the whole crew got quiet and realized what could have happened. The director came over to me and thanked me for such an impressive, professional stunt I had just accomplished.

All I could say to him was, "You're welcome."

The cameraman came over and said, "I want to personally thank you." He was terribly shaken up, thinking what could have happened.

As the crew was wrapping up for the day, they all came over and told me what a great job I had done. As I was coming down the hill as bombs and explosions were going off, I told myself, "Okay, it is time to retire from all of this if I live through this stunt."

I came home and told my wife, Patti, that I wanted to retire and sell the movie ranch. I told her about the close call I had and that I wasn't sure I was going to make it. So I did sell my big movie ranch, and my son, Marcel Rene Veluzat, ran the small 50's Town Ranch I retained.

In the movie business, I have learned to pay attention to my gut feelings. It may be time to retire, as a lot of my stunt buddies have gotten hurt and some killed. As much as I love the movie business and my friends and the excitement of the movies, semiretiring is the right move for me. I still have the 50's Town Movie Ranch that my son manages. I still oversee the ranch and feel the relief of all the pure pressure of getting up at 4:00 a.m. and getting home at 9:00 p.m. in the dark. The joke we all say is, "We never see our house in the daylight." Now I have time to do all the little projects I have put off for twenty years, and now I have time to drive all my exotic cars and go places and just enjoy a little life.

Rene's office

Rene driving a Hummer in a blowup scene

Rene driving a Hummer in a blowup scene

Rene Veluzat and Iron Man

Rene Veluzat Résumé

Education

- Middle Street School, Huntington Park, California
- Henry T. Gage Junior High, Huntington Park, California
- Huntington Park High School, Huntington Park, California
- Woodbury University, Los Angeles, California
- Pierce Junior College, Los Angeles, California

Awards

- Man of the Year of Santa Clarita Valley, 1975
- Vice President of Newhall-Saugus-Valencia Chamber of Commerce, 1975
- Honorary Kentucky Colonel, presented by Governor Wilkins of Kentucky, 1988
- Chamber of Commerce President Award for Outstanding Efforts, 1977
- Outstanding Services to the Community of Santa Clarita Valley, Chamber of Commerce Award, 1976
- Certificate of Honor, "Highest Honors," All-American Boy 1955, presented by Phillip McClay, 1955
- House of Representatives for Dedicated Work to the Santa Clarita Valley, presented by Barry Goldwater Jr., 1975
- The Los Angeles County Award for Dedicated Leader in Numerous Civic Organizations and Activities, presented by Baxter Ward, 1975
- Certificate of Appreciation for the Forty-Eighth Annual Old West Celebration, presented by the president of the Newhall-Saugus-Valencia Chamber of Commerce Women's Division, Florence M. Cheesebrough, 1978
- The Congress of the United States in Special Recognition of Rene Veluzat, presented by Barry Goldwater Jr.
- Certificate of Recognition for Outstanding and Exceptional Personal Service to the Community of the 1977 Chamber Building Program, presented by Senator Lou Cusanovich, Nineteenth Senate California Legislature
- Certificate of Appreciation for Member of the Board of Directors (1975–1977), Newhall-Saugus-Valencia Chamber of Commerce, presented by Richard Milar (president)
- Resolution presented by the Honorable Robert C. Cline, Thirty-Seventh Assembly District
- Newhall-Saugus-Valencia Chamber of Commerce for Dedicated Service beyond the Call of Duty, 1977
- Commendation from the Senate California Legislature Resolution of the Rules Committee, presented by Senator Newton R. Russell, 1975

Accomplishments and Trainings

- Actor since 1950
- Teamster Local 399 studio driver, 1978
- General contractor since 1978
- Licensed private investigator, 1980
- Private Airman Third Class, helicopters and airplanes, 1990
- Member California Horse Racing Board as a thoroughbred racehorse owner, 1972
- Private patrol operator, owner of Titanium Protection, 1980
- California Security Training Academy graduate, 1980
- Professional Firearms Qualification Training, 1982
- Ordained minister for the Progressive Universal Life Church, 1998
- Member of Newhall-Saugus Rotary Club
- Member of the Santa Clarita Valley Chamber of Commerce, 1974
- Member of the Harley-Davidson Owners Club
- Owner of three movie ranch locations
- Presently owner of one movie ranch, a fifty-six-acre location with a complete '50s town, gas station, diner bar, and paved streets (Veluzat.com)
- Owner of Mexican Town Movie Ranch, March 23, 2007
- Owner and trainer of thoroughbred racehorses in Hollywood Park, Santa Anita, and Del Mar Racetracks, with Willie Shoemaker as my jockey
- Still very much involved in the business of my 50's Town Movie Ranch.

KEVIN KARZIN/The Signal

Rene Veluzat shows off the latest addition to his collection of movie memorabilia — Roy Rogers' gun set. The movie ranch owner plans to display pistols above the mantle of his Newhall home.

A Piece of Movie History

That's what Rene Veluzat took home from a recent charity auction

By HEIDI GESIRIECH
Signal Staff Writer

We all know what happened to Roy Rogers' famous horse, Trigger. But have you ever wondered what happened to that beautiful gun set worn by the famous cowboy in his early films? You know, the ones that every little boy in the 1950s had to have a likeness of?

Those guns, complete with their holsters and bullets, are hanging encased in glass above the mantle in the Newhall home of local movie ranch owner, Rene Veluzat.

Veluzat purchased the gun set July 19 during a silent auction at the Golden Boot Awards in Los Angeles for $2,300.

Veluzat has been a longtime fan of Roy Rogers, and even met him as a child and later at the singing cowboy's museum in Apple Valley, but never expected to ever own such a piece of memorabilia.

The silent auction at the Golden Boot Awards ceremony is a fund-raiser for the Motion Picture and Television Fund Foundation. Veluzat has been attending the awards show for five years.

"I'm a collector of things," stated Veluzat. "Last year I missed the silent auction, so this year my wife and I decided we'd get there early. Besides, the money goes to charity."

Bidding started on the Roy Rogers gun set at $1,000. After writing his name down on the bidding sheet, Veluzat realized he wasn't alone in his quest of ownership. Actress Anne Jeffreys, who was being honored that night, was bidding on the same gun set, as well as an automatic pistol used by John Wayne.

Jeffreys really wanted the John Wayne gun and Veluzat had more interest in the Rogers' set, so the two made a deal to stop bidding on the others' preferences. When the bidding closed, they each walked away with their guns of choice.

The 1938 limited edition gun set authorized by Roy Rogers from the Early Years Series is just another item Veluzat has added to a memorabilia collection spanning 45 years in the entertainment industry.

Veluzat, 56, and his two younger brothers were born and raised in the Santa Clarita Valley on a 750-acre cattle ranch, owned by their father, near the corner of Haskell Canyon and Copper Hill. The house they grew up in is gone, but the land has been subdivided and now contains a variety of well-known and often-used movie sets and props, owned by the Veluzat family.

The old Mexican town, with sets built by Veluzat himself, has been used in numerous films and television shows, including the "The A Team," "Dukes of Hazzard," "Knots Landing," "Don Juan

DeMarco" with Johnny Depp, "Mr. Wrong" with Ellen DeGeneres, and music videos by Madonna and Bon Jovi.

Veluzat has a photo album and hallway chocked full of photos reflecting a lifetime of work on movies and television. At age 10, he was discovered by a talent agent during a guitar recital and as they say in the business, the rest is history.

He went on to act and perform stuntwork for such television shows as "Wagon Train," "The Ozzie and Harriet Show," "Laredo," and "My Three Sons," as well as such movies as "The Shakiest Gun in the West" with Don Knotts, "The Chase" with Marlon Brando, 10 Elvis Presley films, the "Planet of the Apes" series and all of the beach party flicks with Annette Funicello and Frankie Avalon.

Today, Veluzat is involved in another project. He gave over 20 acres of his father's land in Saugus to create a brand new movie studio. He celebrated the grand opening July 5.

While he will remain a partner in the Saugus movie ranch with his father and brothers, Renaud and Andre, who also own Melody Ranch in Newhall, he is proud to call his new movie ranch the "Rene Veluzat Motion Picture Ranch" and he will maintain 100 percent ownership.

"This past year extreme advanced opportunity came my way to break away

from the family business and start my own," explained Veluzat. "We built a studio with a Western street, complete with a farm house and barn, and a total urban town."

The urban town opened with a bang, literally, while being used for the shooting of one episode of a new T.V. series, "Soldier of Fortune." Various cars and buildings, including the rustic gas station, were exploded during the filming, but not a scratch was left on his set, said Veluzat.

The new "Andy Griffith-like" town, which could be Anywhere, U.S.A., comes complete with a paved street, real fire hydrants and street lights, a rustic gas station, large diner, biker bar, bank, hardware store, police station, motel, and miscellaneous other small buildings.

With a host of colorful stories from his past, Veluzat is busy compiling his memoirs and hopes to have them published in the near future. He says he plans to donate a portion of the proceeds from his book to charity.

"I just want to say thank you to all of the people who have helped me get to where I am today," said Veluzat. "I didn't want to take guitar lessons, but my mother made me, I didn't want to be in that first show, but my mother made me. And I never thought of being in movies, but the talent agent told my parents their boys should be in films. It's amazing how it's all just happened."

168

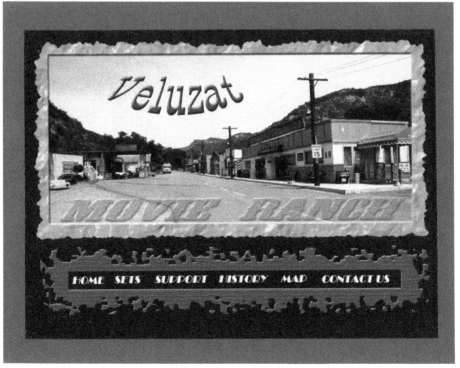

That's a Wrap

IN THE MOVIE business, the director calls action, and at the end of the scene, he calls out, "Cut! Check the gate," meaning check the camera to see if everything is good, no dust or anything on the film.

Then the camera operator calls out, "Good, check."

The director calls out, "Print it. Okay, folks, that is a wrap for the day."

So it is a wrap on my book. Hope you enjoyed the reading.

Thank you.

The End

About the Author

Rene Veluzat's seventy years of movie experience in all phases of the movie business has led to his writing of this book about funny experiences behind the scenes with famous movie stars.

CPSIA information can be obtained
at www.ICGtesting.com
Printed in the USA
BVHW022307130421
604820BV00010B/804

9 781662 418617